S O L I D
FOUNDATION
for
CHRISTIANITY

Deguol Mawunya Sempere

Solid Foundation for Christianity

*The perfect foundation to serve
God in Spirit and in truth*

ISBN 978-434-265-4657

Copyright @ 2023 Truth Announced Global Publishing

*Truth Announced
Global Publishing*

This page was intentionally left blank

Contents

Introduction

The Bible is a very powerful book that remains relevant till eternity. The message of the Bible has helped many people live a victorious life when they study it in its proper context. At the same time, studying the Bible in the wrong context also brought many into terrible beliefs that opened room for evil spirits to find their way into their lives and homes and ultimately put them in bondage.

The Bible is a spiritual book; it's not a literal book like many thinks. To understand the message of the Bible, you need to be taught as its understanding is not open to everybody. The natural man is blinded to the message of Bible until he will his life to Christ and begins to receive teachings of the Word of God. That is why you must attend church to be taught the Word of God. Don't deceive yourself; you can't study the Bible and fully understand it all by yourself. People say they just want to read their bible and pray to God on their own without going to church. They believe the Holy Spirit will teach them the Bible. Well, that is not right, the Holy Spirit doesn't teach people that way; he wouldn't have asked us to go church.

Hebrews 10:25 NLT And let us not neglect our meeting together (church), as some people do, but encourage one another, especially now that the day of his return is drawing near.

That verse reveals God's concern against those who don't go or skip church services. You are about to receive some great teaching from this book. This book was inspired by the deep teachings I received from the Spirit of God through the ministry of the man of God, Pastor Chris Oyakhilome D.Sc. DSc. DD. It's written to help you understand the person, character and nature of God and Christianity better. With that understanding, you will be set free and prepared for a victorious life. You will also be prepared against deception and false teachings. This book will guide you through the core of Christianity and help solidify your faith in God.

As we all know, a solid foundation is the key to a successful life. Be it business, education, or life as a whole. The same solid foundation is needed for a victorious Christian life. Unfortunately, that is what most Christians lack. Through this book, the Spirit of God will help you understand and lay for you a great foundation. Take your time to study the book.

In case you have any questions or need clarity on any subject, reach us at the following email: truthannounced@gmail.com; Deguols@yahoo.com

Chapter One

The Pre-Adamic World

When you study your bible very well, you will notice that Genesis chapter 1 is not the beginning of the universe. Besides the information given in the Bible about that, so many other scientific proofs validate that. When you calculate the age of the earth from Genesis to date, you will realise it doesn't tally with many scientific findings. That means, there is more the Bible is silent on.

The writer of the book of Genesis (Moses) knew about the pre-adamic world (the world before Adam), but he just decided to stay focused on his main subject which is the human race from Adam. So, he just gave a brief general introduction to the creation of the universe with planet earth as his main focus since this is where man lives. Some people say "there was no world before Adam." They don't believe in the pre-Adamic world. Well, the nice thing is whether or not there was a world before Adam, it doesn't affect anyone's salvation. Salvation is not based on faith in the pre-Adamic world but faith in Jesus Christ, the Son of God.

In this chapter, I will briefly introduce the revelations I have about the pre-Adamic world and I believe after reading it, you will receive a great insight. I will only discuss the role of Lucifer, his angels, and his fall in connection to the pre-Adamic world. In case you are still not convinced after reading, don't worry, keep reading the book, there are lots of beautiful things the Spirit of God will teach you.

Pre-adamic world means the world before Adam; the first man God created. The subject of the pre-Adamic world has to do with the world and events before Adam. Let's start our subject with the verse below.

Genesis 1:1 In the beginning God <u>created</u> the heaven and the earth.

When you critically look at the verse above, it suggests something very important. Look at the underlined word; it's in the past tense. That means the heaven and the earth that was created in the verse were completed. It says "in the beginning, God created not God was creating" When you are creating something, and it's not yet done, you don't say "you have created"; you say "you are creating". Millions of years back, God created the heaven and this earth. Both were created at almost the same moment. Both geographical locations were completed and functioning well. After several years, something happened to the earth, and the Genesis 1:2 came to play.

Genesis 1:2 <u>And</u> the earth was without form and void, and darkness was upon the face of the deep. And the Spirit of God moved upon the face of the waters.

Even though there is a conjunction "and" in between the two verses above, they are not directly connected like many would read it. There are several years in between the two verses. We are told in verse 1 that the earth was created; in verse 2, we are told the same earth that was created in verse 1, is now without form and void. But as you know, you don't say you created something which is without form and void. That suggests something might have happened to the earth that was created to make it formless and void. Yes, something indeed happened to the earth, which brought about the formlessness. Let's look into what happened to that beautiful earth God created.

When God created the earth in verse 1, everything was beautiful and glorious. The earth was functioning well, and everything was going well as planned by God. Some people were in the earth then, but I believe they didn't have the same image like us. Lucifer, who later became Satan the Devil, was the angel God assigned to be in charge of the earth.

He was given an assignment by God to control all the activities of the earth and to ensure God's will was done in the earth. He was God's representative here in the earth. In fact, for many years, Lucifer did a marvellous job on that assignment. The responsibility was so great that Lucifer was given almost one-third of the heavenly angels to work under him here in the earth. Today, we still have hosts of angels working with the Holy Spirit in the earth.

Lucifer was beautifully created for this special assignment. He was equipped with everything he needed for the job. Let's look at Lucifer's description addressed in the figure of the king of Tyre.

Ezekiel 28:12-15 NIV Son of man, take up a lament concerning the king of Tyre and say to him: 'This is what the Sovereign Lord says: "You were the seal of perfection, full of wisdom and perfect in beauty. [13] You were in Eden, the garden of God; every precious stone adorned you: carnelian, chrysolite and emerald, topaz, onyx and jasper, lapis lazuli, turquoise and beryl. Your settings and mountings were made of gold; on the day you were created, they were prepared. [14] You were anointed as a guardian cherub, for so I ordained you. You were on the holy mount of God; you walked among the fiery stones. [15] You were blameless in your ways from the day you were created till wickedness was found in you.

Isaiah 14:12-16 How art thou fallen from heaven, O Lucifer, son of the morning! how art thou cut down to the ground, which didst weaken the nations! [13] <u>For thou hast said in thine heart, I will ascend into heaven,</u> I will exalt my throne above the stars (the angels, creatures) of God: I will sit also upon the mount of the congregation, in the sides of the north: [14] <u>I will ascend above the heights of the clouds;</u> I will be like the most high.

Where was Lucifer going to ascend from? He was going to ascend from the earth; because he was in the earth, not heaven. You don't ascend when you are already in heaven. Some people say Lucifer was the choir leader in heaven. No verse suggests that He was created with musical instruments but the Bible said nothing about his musical ministry in heaven. While Lucifer was carrying out his duties here in the earth, I believe he was carried away by the authority God had given him. He couldn't believe such a great domain was given to him to control. He thought "Why can't I just take over heaven as well and have everything totally under my control," he thought he had everything it takes to overthrow God. He made all the angels working under him aware of his plan. Now, after Lucifer got the allegiance of his angels, he set a day to ascend with them to heaven to overthrow God. Lucifer already had the right to ascend to heaven anytime he wanted and had been doing that.

The day came, and he led the host of these angels to heaven to help him fight God and his angels. The archangel Michael one of the angels of war observed that Lucifer's visit to heaven this particular time was not for good. He quickly gathered his angels (angels of war in heaven), and they fought against Lucifer and his angels defeated and prevented them from entering heaven. Lucifer couldn't enter heaven with his angels.

Revelation 12:7-9 And there was war in heaven: Michael and his angels fought against the dragon (Lucifer), and the dragon fought and his angels (the angels with him in the earth), ⁸ And prevailed not; neither was their place found any more in heaven. ⁹ And the great dragon was cast out, that old serpent, called the Devil, and Satan, which deceiveth the whole world: he was cast out into the earth, and his angels were cast out with him.

When Lucifer lost that battle, he lost his place and rights in heaven as well and therefore was cast down to the earth. Why wasn't he cast to any other planet but the earth? I've heard many people raise concern and ask questions like, "why would God cast Lucifer (who became Satan) to the earth where his children are when he couldn't accommodate him in heaven?" God never cast Lucifer down to the earth. Lucifer was in the earth, he made his evil plans when he was here in the earth, not in heaven. He ascended to heaven from the earth. Some people say Lucifer planned evil against God in heaven. That is not true; he couldn't plan evil in heaven. Nobody could plan evil in heaven. In heaven, it's only the will of God that is done, unlike the earth, where everybody has their own will. When Lucifer and his angels ascended to heaven and couldn't prevail, they returned to the earth. Which earth am I talking about here? This very earth we live in today, but this event happened far before Adam was created.

When Lucifer returned to the earth, he corrupted himself, his power, wisdom and knowledge and became Satan, the Devil. I hope that answers the question, "Why did God create Satan?" God didn't create Satan; he created Lucifer, and Lucifer corrupted himself to become Satan the Devil. His beauty before his corruption was described for us in Ezekiel 28:12-15. Let's look at his description after his corruption.

Ezekiel 28:16-19 Lucifer, through your widespread trade you were filled with violence, and you sinned. So I drove you in disgrace from the mount of God, and expelled you, guardian cherub, from among the fiery stones. ¹⁷ Your heart became proud on account of your beauty, and you corrupted your wisdom because of your splendor. So I threw you to the earth; I made a spectacle of you before kings. ¹⁸ By your many sins and dishonest trade you have desecrated your sanctuaries. So I made a fire come out from you, and it consumed you, and I reduced you to ashes on the ground in the sight of all who were watching. ¹⁹ All the nations who knew you are appalled at you; you have come to a horrible end and will be no more.'"

Lucifer didn't only corrupt himself; he also corrupted everything God placed under him here in the earth. He corrupted all of God's creation to the point that the original of anything was hard to find, so God destroyed the earth with water and total darkness. I am not talking about Noah's flood here. Noah's flood happened years after Adam was created, but this particular destruction of the earth occurred before Adam was created. That's what Genesis 1:2 was referring to. The event I spoke about happened between Genesis 1:1 and Genesis 1:2.

In Genesis 1:1, the earth was created and functioning well until Lucifer corrupted it and caused God to destroy it with water and darkness. That was what made the earth created in verse 1 without form and void as described in verse 2 because it was destroyed. The water God used to destroy the earth is what we have today as the sea. Satan and his evil angels couldn't die when God destroyed the earth because they are spirit beings, and spirits don't die.

Let's look at another verse with reference to the pre-adamic world. I will quote it from different versions for a better understanding.

Jeremiah 4:23-26 MSG I looked at the earth it was back to <u>pre-Genesis chaos</u> <u>and emptiness</u>. I looked at the skies, and <u>not a star to be seen</u> (darkness). I looked at the mountains they were trembling like

aspen leaves, And all the hills rocking back and forth in the wind. I looked—what's this! <u>Not a man or woman in sight</u> (total destruction), and not a bird to be seen in the skies. I looked—this can't be! Every garden and orchard shriveled up. All the towns were ghost towns. And all this because of God, because of the blazing anger of God.

A careful examination of the verses above shows it's not talking about the flood of Noah. Have you noticed the underlined phrases are closely related to Genesis 1:2. Compare the two verses below.

Genesis 1:2 And the earth <u>was without form, and void</u>; and <u>darkness</u> was upon the face of the deep. And the Spirit of God moved upon the face of the waters.

Jeremiah 4:23 (KJV) I beheld the earth, and, lo, <u>it was without form, and void</u>; and the heavens, and they had <u>no light</u> (darkness). [24] I beheld the mountains, and, lo, they trembled, and all the hills moved lightly. [25] I beheld, and, lo, <u>there was no man</u>, and all the birds of the heavens were fled. [26] I *beheld, and, lo, the fruitful place was a wilderness, and all the cities thereof were broken down at the presence of the Lord, and by his fierce anger.*

There is no time in history those verses could be referring to except the pre-adamic world. The scope of this chapter is to introduce you to the pre-adamic world and the origin of Satan. The introduction will also help you understand several other biblical concepts.

I believe you've got enough information from the above introduction to understand the pre-adamic world. You now know who Lucifer was and how he became Satan. As you continue to study the Word of God to a higher level, you will need the knowledge you got from the pre-adamic world to explain and answer certain questions. God bless you as you continue to read the book.

Chapter Two
The Creation of Man

In the previous chapter, we discussed how Lucifer was cast out of heaven and back to the earth. We also discussed how Lucifer corrupted himself and all other things in the earth causing God to destroy the earth with water and darkness. After everything was fully destroyed to the satisfaction of God, He decided to recreate the earth again. The earth as a planet wasn't destroyed; it was the things inside it that were destroyed.

Genesis 1:2 says the Spirit of God began to move upon the face of the waters, and God commanded light into being. I want you to note that the light in Genesis 1:3 was not the sun but God manifesting himself as light. The sun was later created in verse 16. You can read Genesis 1:3-25 by yourself to see how the earth was recreated.

The creation story we have in Genesis 1 is not the creation of the world but the recreation. I showed you above how the earth was created and destroyed before the days of Genesis. Spend a good time to read the beautiful recreation story of the earth. When God was done recreating the earth, he decided to create a creature that would head the whole of his creation, which is man. Let's begin to look at how man was created.

Genesis 1:26 Then God said, "Let <u>Us</u> make man in Our <u>image</u>, according to Our <u>likeness</u>; let them have dominion over the fish of the sea, over the birds of the air, and over the cattle, over all the earth and over every creeping thing that creeps on the earth.

After everything had been restored, God the Father said, this time, let us make man in our image and after our likeness. That suggests, the first people from the pre-adamic world were not in the image of God. What God meant in that verse was to make someone who looks like him to represent him before the creation and the creation before him. This time, God won't allow an angel to rule the earth anymore like he did in the first earth. He wants a creation who is exactly like him to rule over the earth now. From that same verse, I want us to examine those keywords underlined.

The word "Us" in the verse is Elohim, the plural form of God, which refers to the Godhead. At this particular time, the Godhead comprises God the Father, the Spirit, and the Word. There was no Jesus at this time. From the scriptures, the Godhead has been described in different ways according to the dispensation. Let's look at an example below.

1 John 5:7 For there are three that bear record in heaven, <u>the Father</u>, <u>the Word</u>, and the <u>Holy Ghost</u>: and these three are one.

Can you see a perfect description of the Godhead in that verse without Jesus? There was a time when there was no Jesus. He came into existence when he was born of Mary. Until Jesus was born by Mary, he wasn't in heaven or anywhere in the spirit realm.

John 1:1-5,14, In the beginning, was <u>the Word</u>, and the Word was with God, and the Word was God. ² The same was in the beginning with God. ³ All things were made by him (the Word), and without him (the Word) was not anything made that was made. ⁴ In him (the Word) was life; and the life was the light of men. ⁵ And the light shineth in darkness; and the darkness comprehended it not. ¹⁴ And <u>the Word became flesh</u>, and dwelt among us, (and we beheld his glory, the glory as of the only begotten of the Father,) full of grace and truth.

Verses 1-5 gave us a beautiful story about the Word of God. Throughout those verses, he was talking about the Word, not Jesus. It spoke of how He was in the very beginning with God and made all things. It described how the Word carries life which serves as light for men. In verse 14, we are told that the Word became flesh. In other words, the Word put on flesh; the Word became a human being. When the Word became flesh, he was named Jesus (the

Son). Jesus is the Word of God in human flesh. We call him "the Son of God" Son of God means God in human flesh. It doesn't mean God giving birth to a baby boy. Before Jesus was born by the virgin Mary, he was the Word of God. From Genesis 1:26 when the Father said let "us" make man verse 26, the Father was talking to the Spirit and the Word.

The next word to examine from Genesis 1:26 is "**Image**" We all know we were created in the image of God. "Image" here is not referring to our outward look, which is the body; it is talking about our spirit beings. Our spirits are the ones created in the image of God. You may say "what about our bodies" With our physical look, we have some that are male and others that are female. God is neither male nor female; God is a spirit, and spirits are genderless. We don't have a male spirit or a female spirit. We only have male and female features in the body, and the sole reason is for reproduction. All spirits (Satan, demons, angels, humans, Godhead) are all genderless. If you are a man reading this book, your spirit is not a male; you are only a male in the body, and if you are a lady reading this book, your spirit is not a female; you only have female features on your body. That's why Jesus said in *Mathew 22:30* that, when we get to heaven, there will be no marriage; we will be like the angels, which are neither male nor female. So, when God said to create man in his image, he was referring to man's spirit, not man's body. The beauty and quality of your spirit are the same as the quality of your words. Great words, produce good quality spirit.

The next word is **Likeness**. God said to create man in his image and his likeness. Man, in the likeness of God means man to function like God. God created man to look like him and to function like him. Man was created with many abilities to function like God. Because God created man to create just like him, he only created the raw materials for man and expected man to continue with creation. The complete recreation of this world is to be done by man. God didn't create tables, houses, or cars for man; He created the raw materials and expected man to fashion them into any shape of his choice.

So, who is man? ***Man is a spirit being who has a soul and lives in the body.*** Every human being is primarily a spirit. You are not your body; your body is just the house in which you live. The real you is your spirit. Knowing that man is a spirit helps you to relate with people with caution. Find out the characteristics of a spirit, and that enables you to understand yourself and others.

Genesis 1:27: So God <u>created</u> man in his own image, in the image of God he created him; male and female he created them.

God did create man in his image and likeness, as he proposed in verse Genesis 1:26. The creation of man in the verse above is the creation of the spirits of Adam and Eve. Even though the verse says God created a male and a female, it doesn't suggest God created male and female spirits. God created two genderless spirits intending to form one as male and the other as female. God blessed them and charged them to multiply and fill the earth. He charged them to be in charge of all his creation. Since man has been created as a spirit being and the earth is a physical realm, man couldn't function here in the earth, and God had to do something about that. Man needed a physical body to function in the earthly realm. Let's look at what God did about that.

Genesis 2:7 And the LORD God <u>formed man</u> of the dust of the ground, and breathed into his nostrils the breath of life; and man became a living soul.

The above verse is talking about the same person created in Genesis 1:27. The verse above talks about the formation of the body of man and the one in Genesis 1:27 talks about the creation of man. You soon know the difference. Man was first created and then formed. The spirit of man was created, and the body of man was formed. Concerning the spirit of man, the term "created" was used, but the term "formed" was used concerning the body of man. That is very important and reveals something to us.

To **create** means to bring into existence from nothing that is already existing. God is the raw material of man's spirit. The spirit of man was created from nothing already existing in this world. To **form** something, on the other hand, means to bring into existence from an already existing material. It means to fashion an existing material into another shape. For example, a table was formed from wood and man's body was formed from clay.

The spirit of man needed a body to enable him to function in the earth. This is because no spirit is allowed to carry out physical activity in the earth without being in a physical body. That is why all evil spirits seek to possess people. The reason is they need a human body to carry out their evil agendas. Same way the spirit man God created cannot also function in the earth without a body. So, God formed the body of man from the dust of the ground (clay) and breathed into his nostrils the breath of life (the spirit he created), and man became a living soul (the spirit plus the body). Now man can move and talk.

That man was Adam.

Genesis 2:8 And the LORD God planted a garden eastward in Eden; and there he put the man whom he had formed

God didn't just leave the man to find his way out. He planted a garden for him. God arranged a special place for Adam. He planted some trees for food, and others for beauty. Don't think God commanded the garden down from heaven. He planted the garden. That means every plant took its normal time to grow. God needed to wait for the garden to grow before he brought Adam into it.

When the garden was ready, God invited Adam to be introduced to the garden. He took him into the garden and showed him everything and how he was free to eat from the fruits of the trees in the garden. God took him further and showed him a particular tree in the middle of the garden, and commanded him not to eat of that tree. He also made him understand the outcome if he disobeyed and ate the fruit.

Genesis 2:15-17 And the Lord God took the man, and put him into the garden of Eden to dress it and to keep it. [16] And the Lord God commanded the man, saying, of every tree of the garden thou mayest freely eat: [17] But of the tree of the knowledge of good and evil, thou shalt not eat of it: for in the day that thou eatest thereof thou shalt surely die.

Take note of something here, God gave that instruction, particularly to Adam. He was to keep the garden and dress it. The garden was the place Adam would start his government from, to the rest of the earth. He was to make the garden more comfortable where more lives could flourish. Adam followed God's instruction and lived in the garden happily for at least three years before the next verse.

Genesis 2:18 And the Lord God said, It is not good that the man should be alone; I will make him a help meet for him (a helper).

God saw that Adam was alone, not lonely. Adam wasn't lonely; he was alone. Alone about what?

Alone about the assignment God gave him to keep the garden and dress it (Genesis 2:15), That was the assignment God gave Adam. God observed that he was alone on the assignment. He was the only person doing that assignment. The animals and the plants weren't helping him. So, God decided to make someone to help him. It's not Adam being alone that brought the idea of Eve. Eve had been created already (*Genesis 1:27*). She was yet to be formed. Even though God created Adam and Eve on the same day, he didn't form their body on the same day. God waited to get a connecting factor to connect Eve to Adam before he formed Eve.

Let's look at the meaning and the difference between these two terms. To be lonely and to be alone. To be alone means exclusive of anyone; to be the only person on the task. For example, you are reading this book alone. That means no other person is reading it with you. On the other hand, being lonely means the absence of fellowship. Adam wasn't lonely because he was in fellowship with God. Loneliness is a thing of the spirit and soul. You can be among a large group of people and still be lonely. Loneliness is disconnection. When you feel lonely, it's not marriage or sex you need; you can have enough of all those and still be lonely. Adam was alone with the assignment God gave him to keep and dress the garden. So, Eve was created to help Adam keep and dress the garden. That was the original reason why Eve was created, to help Adam with the assignment God gave him.

Genesis 2:21-25 And the Lord God caused a deep sleep to fall upon Adam, and he slept: and he took one of his ribs, and closed up the flesh instead thereof; 22 And the rib, which the Lord God had taken from man, made he a woman, and brought her unto the man. 23 And Adam said, this is now bone of my bones, and flesh of my flesh: she shall be called Woman, because she was taken out of Man. 24 Therefore shall a man leave his father and his mother, and shall cleave unto his wife: and they shall be one flesh. 25 And they were both naked, the man and his wife, and were not ashamed.

To form Eve, God took one of the ribs of Adam and used it during the formation. When Eve came, Adam was the one who showed her around and gave her the same instruction God gave him concerning the tree of the knowledge of good and evil. When Eve came into the garden, life got even better in the garden. They lived happily in the garden for several years, and God used to visit and fellowship with them. They lived happily in the garden for 33 years before their fall in Genesis 3.

Chapter Three
The Fall of Man

After the creation of Eve, the couple lived in the garden for 33 years then Genesis 3 began. One day, a strange figure, the serpent was introduced into the story. That's definitely a figure in rebellion against God.

Genesis 3:1 Now <u>the serpent</u> was more subtil than any beast of the field which the Lord God had made. And <u>he</u> said unto the woman, Yea, hath God said, Ye shall not eat of every tree of the garden?

As we learnt from chapter one, Lucifer had fallen and became Satan, the devil. One day, Satan came into the garden where Adam and Eve were and his plan to was to deceive Adam and Eve to rebel against God, just as he is in rebellion against God. As you learnt, spirits need a physical body to carry out their activities in the earthly realm. When Satan came, he needed a body to relate with Adam and Eve. He couldn't enter Adam or Eve, he then looked through the animals and realised that the serpent had the character he needed to carry out his mission. He entered into it and went to have a conversation with Eve.

The serpent in the verse above refers to the snake with Satan inside it; that's why the serpent is given a personality as "he" in the verse. The serpent went to Eve and said, "Madam, I have observed you and Daddy Adam ate from all the trees in the garden except that tree in the middle of the garden; is it that you don't like the fruit or God warned you guys not to eat of it?" Look at the woman's reply

Genesis 3:2-3 And the woman said unto the serpent, We may eat of the fruit of the trees of the garden: ³ But of the fruit of the tree which is in the midst of the garden, God hath said, Ye shall not eat of it, <u>neither shall ye touch it, lest ye die</u>

The woman replied it's not like we don't like it, but God instructed us not to eat of it. She added that God said they shouldn't even touch it or else they would die. But God never said they shouldn't touch the tree when he instructed Adam in Genesis 2:17. It was Adam who gave her that information that God said they shouldn't touch it. Adam loved Eve and didn't want her to die, so he told her that God said they shouldn't even touch the tree. Of course, if you don't touch it, you won't eat it. But that miscommunication was exactly what led to their fall. When Eve said that to the serpent, the serpent laughed and said, "You guys are still kids; you won't die as God said, he is trying to hide something very important from you and your husband. It's a tree rather for your advantage."

Genesis 3:4-5 And the serpent said unto the woman, Ye shall not surely die: [5] For God doth know that in the day ye eat thereof, then your eyes shall be opened, and ye shall be as gods, knowing good and evil.

The serpent said, "God doesn't want you guys to be like him, and the secret to being like God is in that tree". But we are told in *Genesis 1:27* that they were already created in God's image and likeness. Eve initially didn't fall for Satan's tricks, but the serpent persistent with his gospel to Eve. I want you to know that Satan didn't use a day to deceive Eve. This was something that took quite some time. The serpent repeatedly talked about the tree until the woman's eyes opened to some details.

Genesis 3:6 And <u>when the woman saw</u> that the tree was good for food and that it was pleasant to the eyes, and a tree to be desired to make one wise, she took of the fruit thereof, and did eat, and also gave unto her husband with her, and he did eat.

Look at what happened in the verse above. When the woman "saw", though she had been in the garden with the tree for 33 years, she only saw those details when Satan spoke about the tree. Yes, Satan had now opened her eyes to things she shouldn't know.

This is how Satan deceived Eve. When the serpent kept talking about the fruit of the tree and the benefits but Eve wasn't falling for the idea, he decided to take it to the next level. He invited Eve to the tree and said, "God said you guys shouldn't eat nor touch it, right?" The woman said "yes". Recall the woman said "God said they shouldn't even touch it", right? The serpent was like touch it and see if anything will happen to you. The woman touched the fruit and realised that nothing happened. All Eve knew was she would die when she touched the fruit. As you know, God never said they shouldn't touch it, so she won't die by touching it. When Eve realised that nothing happened when she touched it, she was also convinced that nothing would happen when she ate the fruit. She then went ahead and ate the fruit.

What happened to her after? Nothing happened. Eve didn't die, she didn't go naked, she didn't lose her connection with God. Nothing happened to Eve. Nothing was supposed to happen to Eve; God never gave any instruction to Eve; the instruction was given to Adam. When Eve realised nothing happened after she ate the fruit, she quickly went to Adam, and she was like, "Babe, I have found the truth; God lied to us" Adam was like, "the truth about what?" She said, "We won't die if we eat the fruit of the tree of knowledge of Good and Evil," Adam said "No! Don't doubt God." Eve said, "But I've already eaten it, and nothing happened". She also took Adam to the tree and convinced him to eat. Adam also resisted and refused to rebel against God. Adam didn't eat the fruit the same day Eve ate it. For several days, the fruit became Eve's favourite food; she made fruit juice and fruit salad with it almost every day (dramatic narration, right?) Adam observed that Eve had been eating this fruit for several days now, and nothing happened to her, so he was also convinced that nothing would surely happen to him when he ate it as well.

One day, he decided to taste the fruit of the Tree of Knowledge of Good and Evil. Immediately he had a taste; everything changed for both of them. Their eyes opened, and they noticed they were naked. The animals they used to play with began to chase them, trees started growing thorns. When did all these things happen? When Adam ate the fruit, not when Eve ate it. Eve went naked when Adam ate the fruit, not when she ate it. The narration above sounds a little dramatic, but that was exactly what happened.

Genesis 3:7 And the eyes of them both were opened, and they knew that they were naked, and they sewed fig leaves together, and made themselves aprons.

When they realised they had made a blunder of their lives, they started looking for a solution to the problem. They had to use leaves for clothes, imagine. God saw what had happened and came down to find solution to the problem.

Genesis 3:8-11 And they heard the voice of the Lord God walking in the garden in the cool of the day: and Adam and his wife hid themselves from the presence of the Lord God amongst the

trees of the garden. ⁹And the Lord God called unto Adam, and said unto him, Where art thou? ¹⁰And he said, I heard thy voice in the garden, and I was afraid, because I was naked; and I hid myself. ¹¹And he said, who told thee that thou wast naked? Hast thou eaten of the tree, whereof I commanded thee that thou shouldest not eat?

God came into the garden and asked Adam a series of questions. When God ask a question, it's not because he doesn't know the answer; he wants to draw your attention to something. He wants you to know something is wrong. He asked Adam, "Where are you?" It means Adam is not where he is supposed to be. He asked Jacob, "What's your name?" to mean something was wrong with his name. God asked Adam if he ate of the tree he commanded him not to eat; instead of Adam saying, "Yes, I'm sorry," he started blaming games. He blamed God for giving him a woman who was not good enough and caused his downfall.

Genesis 3:12 And the man said, The woman whom thou gavest to be with me, she gave me of the tree, and I did eat.

Adam is trying to say he is not to be blamed because he never did anything nasty when he was alone in the garden. Besides, he doesn't remember requesting a woman. God brought him a woman who caused all these problems. Adam is now blaming God for a wrong choice of partner. When Adam blamed God for the wrong choice of partner, God decided not to give a wife to anybody again. He gave the power to every man to make a choice of his own. When a man finds one he thinks is the best for him, he takes her to God to join them together and after that, there is no coming out. If God's choice is not good, is it man's choice that will be good? Just think about it. Wrong choices are the reason for the challenges in marriages today. God does recommend; he can open your eyes to people he knows could be good for you, but the final decision lies with you. After Adam blamed God, the next time he spoke about marriage was in ***Proverbs 18:22 He who finds a*** *wife finds a good thing and obtains favor from the LORD.*

He who finds a wife, not he whom I give a wife. If you find one, he will give his blessings and favour. He doesn't want to be blamed again. Adam gave the blame to God and Eve for his disobedience. He never took responsibility for his fault.

Genesis 3:13 And the Lord God said unto the woman, what is this that thou hast done? And the woman said, the serpent beguiled me, and I did eat.

God turned to Eve and asked her the meaning of what she did; instead of her also apologising, she gave the blame to the serpent. What Adam and Eve failed to understand was that, an explanation makes no sense when you are at fault. Instead of explaining your point, start finding a solution to the problem.

Chapter Four

The Curse of Man and the Reversal

In this chapter, we will examine the curse Adam and Eve brought upon themselves and the whole human race through disobedience. We will discuss the consequences of the curse and how God reversed the curse. In the previous chapter, we studied how Adam and Eve refused to admit they were wrong. Each of them blamed someone else for their actions. What was God's reaction and what did he do about the situation? Let's go in for the details.

Genesis 3:14-15 And the Lord God said unto the serpent because thou hast done this, thou art cursed above all cattle, and above every beast of the field; upon thy belly shalt thou go, and dust shalt thou eat all the days of thy life: 15 And I will put enmity between thee and the woman, and between thy seed and her seed; it shall bruise thy head, and thou shalt bruise his heel.

Have you noticed God didn't ask the serpent any questions about why he deceived them? He didn't ask the serpent any questions like he asked Adam and Eve. No need to ask the serpent any questions because God knew who was behind the serpent. In verses 14 and 15, God addresses the serpent.

Those words to the serpent are prophetic languages. They are not literally referring to the serpent (a snake). God said the serpent would eat dust for the rest of his life, but snakes don't eat dust; they are carnivores (animals that eat flesh). God said he would walk on his belly for the rest of his life, so people believe snakes had legs until the curse. Snakes were created the way they are today; they had no legs from the very beginning. God wasn't speaking those words to the snake; he was addressing Satan in the serpent. Since Adam and Eve had no idea of who was behind the serpent, God had to speak a language they would understand to address Satan. Since this book is for beginners, I will not explain the meaning of those words to the serpent in this book. At least from verse 15, I hope you can see the prophecy of Christ defeating Satan at the expense of his life.

Genesis 3:16 Unto the woman he said, I will greatly multiply thy sorrow and thy conception; in sorrow thou shalt bring forth children; and thy desire shall be to thy husband, and he shall rule over thee.

Usually, when people read the verse above, they only see the pain during birth. That verse has a lot more to say than that. God didn't say I will give you great sorrow; he said he would greatly multiply her sorrow. It's the sorrow of Eve that will be multiplied. From her disobedience, she brought sorrow upon herself. Eve's curse concerns her childbearing life and her marital life. She may feel pain during birth, but for a woman to die during childbirth is not part of the curse. A woman's death during pregnancy and birth is always coupled with the mistake of mishandling somewhere. Even animals don't die during conception. It is highly unacceptable for a woman to die during birth.

Many ask, is a woman still under that curse after being born again? God has done something about the curse, not just because a woman is born again. Since the curse of Eve has to do with her childbearing and marital life, in reversing the curse, God has to use the husband or the father to reverse it.

1 Timothy 2:13-15 For Adam was first formed, then Eve. [14] And Adam was not deceived, but the woman being deceived was in the transgression. [15] <u>Notwithstanding, she shall be saved in childbearing</u>, if they continue in faith and charity and holiness with sobriety

Ephesians 5:22-24 Wives, submit to your own husbands, as to the Lord. [23] For the husband is head of the wife, as also Christ is head of the church; and He is the Savior of the body. [24] Therefore, just as the church is subject to Christ, so let the wives be to their own husbands in everything.

For a woman not to experience the curse God pronounced upon Eve, she has to submit to her husband. I told you what was said in verse 16 is far more than just feeling pain during birth. God intentionally placed the woman under the man for her protection and well-being. Just look at the lives of women who are submitted to their husbands and compare it with those women who rebelled against their husband's authority.

There is safety, joy, provision, direction, guidance and good health in submission. To rebel against your husband is to expose yourself to Satan's attack. Most married women are suffering because they rebelled against their husbands. If they submit to their husbands, most of those problems would end. Of course, I know of wicked men who treat their wives badly even when submitted. That is between them and their God.

What if the woman is not married? She has to be under the authority (submission) of her father. A woman must always be under the authority of a man at every given time. From birth to the time a woman marries, she has to be under the authority and guidance of her father. During the marriage, the father hands that authority to the husband. A woman who is not under the authority of a man at a given time is likely to make a blunder in her life. Most women can confirm that the time they messed up their lives was the time they rebelled against their father or husband. Submission is not a way to punish a woman; it's rather for her benefit. Every man finds joy in a submissive woman and joyfully provides for her.

Genesis 3:17-19 And unto Adam he said, because thou hast hearkened unto the voice of thy wife, and hast eaten of the tree, of which I commanded thee, saying, thou shalt not eat of it: <u>cursed is the ground for thy sake;</u> in sorrow shalt thou eat of it all the days of thy life; ¹⁸ Thorns also and thistles shall it bring forth to thee; and thou shalt eat the

herb of the field; [19] *In the sweat of thy face shalt thou eat bread, till thou return unto the ground; for out of it wast thou taken: for dust thou art, and unto dust shalt thou return.*

Those are the words God spoke to Adam. God didn't curse Adam; he cursed the ground for his sake. In other words, he made the ground yield nothing or very little from very hard work. At first, God provided everything Adam and his wife needed, but now Adam will have to work hard to feed his family. This curse has also been reversed as well. The state of the ground at that time is not the same as the state of the ground today. Let's look at that.

*Genesis 8:21 And the LORD smelled a sweet savour, and the LORD said in his heart, **<u>I will not again curse the ground any more for man's sake</u>**; for the imagination of man's heart is evil from his youth; neither will I again smite any more everything living, as I have done.*

During the days of the curse, the earth produced nothing from very hard work, unlike today. God reversed the curse; the ground is fertile now. Anything you plant will yield fruits. After the flood of Noah, Noah offered an offering that pleased God so much that the best reward he thought to pay back was to reverse the curse he placed on the ground.

Those are the physical impacts of the curse. God also spoke about how they would die if they ate the fruit. They died as God said. That death was spiritual death, which later resulted in physical death. Spiritual death means separation from God. Adam was disconnected from God the moment he ate the fruit. That separation was the main reason God warned him. I will explain why in the next chapters. Let me show you some heartbreaking moments where God was forced by Adam's actions to sack him from the garden.

Genesis 3:22-24 And the Lord God said, Behold, the man is become as one of us, to know good and evil: and now, lest he put forth his hand, and take

also of the tree of life, and eat, and live forever: ²³ *Therefore the Lord God sent him forth from the garden of Eden, to till the ground from whence he was taken.* ²⁴ *So he drove out the man, and he placed at the east of the garden of Eden Cherubims, and a flaming sword which turned every way, to keep the way of the tree of life.*

Above all the curses God pronounced upon them, he had to drive them out of the garden. It's not just about leaving a garden; it's about leaving God's presence, provision, protection and domain. The hardest decision God ever made was to sack them from the garden. God is not sacking them because he wants to punish them, but it's of necessity. He had to sack them for two major reasons.

Reasons For Sacking Adam And Eve From The Garden

The first reason was to prevent them from eating from the Tree of Life. This tree was also in the garden, and eating from it makes you live forever. Man is now a fallen man and needs to be saved. But if God allows them to eat from the Tree of Life, they will live in the fallen state forever. That means man will grow billions of years with their strength gone, muscles dropped, sight dimmed, but no ability to die. Just look at what someone above 100 years looks like, and imagine someone living for over 5000 years and not dead. God had to prevent them from eating the fruit of the Tree of Life to make it possible for man to die. If man can die, then man can be saved because man's salvation must come through death. But if they eat the fruit of the Tree of Life and live forever, then it becomes impossible for man to be saved since the saviour wouldn't be able to die.

The second reason was that Adam abused the "law of provision" The law of provision states that ***"who so ever defines good and evil must provide"*** Before Adam disobeyed God, God defined good and evil. Whatever God said was good for them; they agreed that it was good, and whatever God said was not good for them, they agreed that it wasn't good for them. When they ate the fruit, what they did was they seized power of attorney to define good and evil for themselves. They wouldn't follow God's definition of good and evil anymore. The law states that *"whoever defines good and evil must provide"*. When God defined good and evil, he provided a place and food for them and took responsibility for their well-being, but now that they seized power to define good and evil, they must provide for themselves. That's the second reason God had to sack them out of the garden.

The law of provision also exists in marriages. Have you ever wondered why the man should be the provider in marriage? The man is the one given the right to define good and evil. If the man is the head of the union, he must define good and evil and he must also provide for the union.

Sacking man out of the garden wasn't easy for God; that was the most difficult decision he ever made.

The darkest day for God. Man is fallen, the earth has failed again the second time, Lucifer failed, and Adam also failed. Fellowship is broken, and judgment has set in. God's best friend is fallen; who will God fellowship with again? Man, won't be able to access God's presence again. God had to cast his friend out of his presence anyway.

Chapter Five
The Origin of Religion

From Genesis chapter 4 to chapter 11 you will read about many evil deeds of men that reflect the state of the fallen man. The effect of the fall has been presented in various stories. Cain killing Abel, Lamech marrying more than one and treating them like his property, fallen angels sleeping with daughters of men, the birth of giants, the imagination of man being full of evil continually, the rebellion at the tower of Babel, etc., are all presentations of the effects of the fall. I will recommend the videos of our Torah Classes on YouTube for you to get more understanding. Search Truth Announced Global Torah Classes on YouTube to watch the videos.

From Genesis 3, we discussed the fall of man in detail. We saw how man sinned against God through disobedience. We saw how man entered into the fallen state, and through that sin entered into the world and death through sin. In this chapter, I will introduce you to the origin of religion, the greatest enemy of men and Christianity.

Before we dive into religion, let's refresh our minds from what we have learnt so far. From our line of studies so far, we will define Sin as disobeying God by taking authority into your own hands to define good and evil for yourself instead of God's definition of good and evil. Anytime you do something, believe something or say something contrary to what God had said, you have sinned. What he said is his definition of what he says is good or bad; you doing otherwise is your definition of what you think is good or bad.

A sinner is, therefore, a man who rebels against God and decides to go contrary to God's ways. In this context, a Christian will be defined as a person following and obeying God's definition of good and evil instead of his definition of good and evil. Since we Christians followed God's definition of good and evil, we are at peace with God. We won't be judged for condemnation; we will only be judged for reward. The definitions I gave above are the basic definitions of sin, a sinner and a Christian. Keep reading for a better understanding.

The Birth Of Religion

When Adam left the garden, he lost access to God's presence and fellowship with God. Originally, Adam was created in the state of God. He had some wonderful features he lost at the fall. Before the fall, Adam could see beyond the walls, he could hear from afar, he could tell the temperature of an object without touching it, and he could know what was happening at a place without being there. After the fall, Adam couldn't see or hear beyond the walls and would need all manner of instruments and devices to navigate his way around the world. Adam knew he had lost something; most importantly, the presence of God. He began to look for the way back to the presence of God. By that, he and his descendants worshipped all manner of idols, thinking that maybe through them, they would find their way back to the presence of God. Paul said worshipping those idols is offering services to demons *(1 Corinthians 10:19-20).* Man's search for the way back to the presence of God was what gave birth to religion. Religion is from the days of Adam; It's not starting from our days. Religion is rebellion against God. It's a way of going contrary to the ways of God. Religion is the greatest enemy of Christianity.

Religion has destroyed billions of people and condemned them to hell. Everybody must fear religion by being mindful of what they believe. You will never know you believed the wrong thing until you humble yourself for the Spirit of God to teach you. Religion was what men replaced God's presence with. How sad!

Christianity Is Not A Religion

Most of the time, Christianity is considered one of the world's best religions. It's regarded as the best religion, but that's not true. Christianity is not a religion, even though there is a religion in Christianity. There is a big difference between religion and Christianity. Religion is the complete opposite of Christianity; Satan set up religion to pollute man's mind to walk in rebellion against God.

Difference Between Religion And Christianity

Religion is man's efforts to reach out to God and to please him. It's all of man's assumptions about God and how he feels God should be worshipped. Jesus said they know not what they worshipped *(John 4:22).* No religion will ever reach or please God. Man cannot find the way back to God's presence by himself. If we could reach God through our efforts, there wouldn't be a need for Jesus to come.

Christianity, on the other hand, is God reaching out to man through Jesus Christ. When God realised man couldn't reach him despite the efforts for decades, he sent Jesus to come and show us the way to his presence. When Jesus came, he said, "I am the way" *(John 14:6)*, not "a way" to mean one of the ways. He said, "No man can reach the Father except by him. He made us understand that no man knows the way to the Father except the one who came from Him *(John 3:13)*.

Jesus declared several times that he came from God. He couldn't be the way to the Father if he is not from the Father. That is what proves all other religious leaders wrong. They don't know the way to the Father and can't lead themselves or anybody to the Father. Let me give you a few differences between Christianity and religion in the next page.

Difference Between Religion And Christianity

Religion	Christianity
Religion is man's effort to reach out to God and to please him.	Christianity is God reaching out to man through Jesus Christ.
The worshippers are not in fellowship with the deity they worship *John 4:22*	The worshippers are one with and in constant fellowship with their God. *1 John 1:3*
The religious leaders are dead with no hope of coming back to life.	The leader (Jesus) died, came back to life, and is still alive today, never to die again.
There is no forgiveness. The worshipper has to atone for his sins.	There is forgiveness in the name of Jesus. Our wrongs are forgiven, and no need for us to pay *Luke 24:47*
Religion is a way to rebel and not believe in God. It's a way to reject God's provision *Romans 10:3*	It's accepting God's finished work through Christ and walking in it.
You can only be righteous by living a sin-free life which is impossible.	Christians are righteous because they were born of God.

Can you also conclude from those differences that Christianity is not a religion? Usually, we consider those who don't go to church or the traditionalists as the people who are in rebellion against God. The truth is we have more churches that are into religious worship. A religious church is a church that doesn't worship God according to the scriptures. Christianity is serving God in spirit. You can't know you are into religious worship unless the Holy Spirit opens your eyes to it through the gospel.

Check the church you go to, and check the kind of messages you are being taught. Find out if it's in accordance with the New Testament gospel. You will have a conviction in your spirit that you are at the right or wrong place. Pray to God to help you know if you are into religious worship. Let the Holy Spirit guide you into true Christianity. I pray by the time you finish this book; the Holy Spirit will give you confirmation.

Chapter Six
The Concept of Sin

This chapter intends to introduce you to the subject of sin. Before we get deep into the subject, understand that wrongdoing and sin are not the same. You can sin without doing anything wrong and do something wrong without sinning. I have explained the difference in one of the chapters below. Man only sins against God, but we can wrongs a fellow brother or sister.

Therefore, God is the best person to define sin and his definition is the standard. Man's definition of good and evil varies from one society to another. What is wrong in one society is good in another. It takes the Word of God to understand what sin is. Let's continue to discuss the subject for a better understanding. I know God will help you understand and set you free from every bondage of sin.

Forms of sin

Sin comes in two forms. The nature of sin and the Act of sin. Pay very good attention to the things am going to discuss with you in this section.

I. The Nature Of Sin

Sin is primarily a nature; it's not necessarily what you do or don't do. Sin is a nature a man is born with. Just like you are a guy or a lady by nature, so is sin. I discussed above how Adam was before his fall. He was created with the nature of God. He was made in the image and likeness of God.

When Adam disobeyed, he fell to his senses and lost the nature of God in him. He reduced himself to his senses; a level where he could not contact God. That's how fellowship was broken between God and man. In *Genesis 2:17,* God said to Adam, he would die the day he would eat of the fruit. Death here is spiritual death, which means complete separation from God. It's not like God rejected Adam after his disobedience, but the new nature of Adam couldn't contact God. He has now become a physical being who can only relate to things he can see feel and touch. This new nature of Adam separated him from God, and that is what we call sin; a nature that separates man from God.

Let's recall the definition of sin again; sin is taking authority into your hands to define good and evil instead of God's definition. Adam seized that authority from God. When Adam gave birth, he noticed the children also came with their own authority to define good and evil for themselves. They were born in rebellion against God and their parents. They inherited the fallen nature from their father, Adam. So is every man born today with that same authority to define good and evil for himself.

If you have ever been with a baby, you would understand this better. Little children are very rebellious. When you instruct them not to touch something, it's the very reason why they would touch it. Because inside them is the authority to decide what they think is good for them not what you think is good for them. When you try to prevent them from touching it, they cry, and the meaning of the crying is that they don't see any reason why you should prevent them from exercising the authority they inherited from their grandpa Adam.

Romans 3:23 <u>For all have sinned</u> and fall short of the glory of God.

Romans 5:12 Wherefore, as by one man sin entered into the world, and death by sin; and <u>so death passed upon all men, for that all have sinned:</u>

I always wonder exactly what goes through the minds of people when they read the verses I quoted above with the underlined statement. It's one of my dreams to make everybody understand that part. Now let me explain. We know those verses have something to do with Adam; it is talking about how the transgression of Adam brought sin into every man's life. You will agree that it would be very unfair for someone to eat his fruit, for God to declare everybody a sinner. You can't be punished for someone's offence. Even human beings don't do that; it's not God who will do that. God didn't declare all of Adam's descendants sinners because he sinned. How, then, did we become sinners through his transgression?

As I said before, Adam's disobedience made him develop a new nature (fallen nature, sinful nature), and this nature can't contact God. A man with this Adamic fallen nature has nothing to do with God. Now, remember that Adam had no child before the fall, and he gave birth after the fall. He gave birth to his children when he was already a fallen man. His children were born, and they inherited the fallen nature from their father. When the children were born, Adam noticed two things. First, the children inherited his fallen nature; they also couldn't connect with God. Secondly, the children looked exactly like him (Adam was created, his children were born, but they looked like him *Genesis 5:2-3).*

The new nature Adam developed is what we call the

nature of sin, which brings about death (complete separation from God). That means Adam became a sinner and separated from God. Now that his children were born with the same nature, they were also born sinners and separated from God; that's how his children also became sinners. Till today, every man born into this world is born after the fallen nature of Adam and therefore born a sinner and separated from God. As far as a man is born with the aid of a man and a woman, he is born a sinner. So, sin is a nature a man is born with. Jesus said in *John 3:7 …you must be born again,* why? Because your first birth came with the nature of sin, and the only way you can receive another nature is by another birth.

If a man is born into this world, he is born a sinner, no matter where he is born or how good he may be. There is nothing a man can do to change the nature of sin. No amount of right living can change the nature of sin. That means the sinner doesn't need to start doing the right things to be saved. After all, most people who are not born again don't even necessarily do anything wrong. If we could just be saved by doing the right things, there wouldn't be a need for Jesus to come; God would have just encouraged us to live right. But that wouldn't work. Living a righteous life doesn't make the sinner righteous. For example, if you are born a lady by nature, there is nothing you can do to change that nature. You may dress, talk, walk, behave, and act like a guy. You may even change gender, but you are still a lady by nature. The only way you could be a guy is to be born a guy. Same way, when a man is born with the nature of sin, his right-living can't change that nature. This is why all religions can't please God even though they all encourage right living. You have to be born again to be righteous because righteousness is also a nature that comes from birth.

Let me take you a bit higher. You may be wondering would a baby who hasn't done anything wrong be considered a sinner? Yes, he is a sinner. Would he go to hell when he dies as a baby? Yes, he will. That sounds unfair, right? That is why parents must dedicate their children. Child dedication is the solution to that problem. Refer to my other book, "How to Raise a Child the Way He Should Go", to learn more about child dedication.

Let me discuss a little more about sin. Anybody who is not born again is a sinner. It doesn't matter how good he may be. Sin is a nature within the spirit of a man. It is the nature of sin that causes a person to sin. Apostle Paul spoke about his personal experience with this nature in Romans 7. A man without the nature of sin cannot sin; the same for a man without the nature of righteousness cannot do right.

A man with the nature of sin may choose to live right, but that doesn't make him a righteous man. In the same way, a righteous man (a Christian) may also choose to live an unrighteous life, and that also doesn't make him a sinner. I said sin and righteousness don't come by what you do or don't do. *2 Corinthians 6:14* says do not be equally yoked with unbelievers. As Christians, the bible doesn't permit us to marry unbelievers. The reason has to do with the nature of sin in their spirit. A man who is not born again has Satan as his father and is extremely wicked to the core. A wicked man may choose to act good until they get the perfect opportunity. Due to the wickedness in a man's spirit, which cannot be easily detected by how he looks on the outside, many gifts (gift of discernment, wisdom, common sense, the Holy Spirit) are given to us Christians to navigate our way. Usually, Christians feel they are smarter than the God who knows what's inside the heart of an unbeliever. They ignore everything he says about the unbeliever, only looking with their physical eyes, get into a relationship with them and the result is usually not a good one. Many got their lives destroyed, and others found themselves in hell due to their association with unbelievers.

The only way the sinful nature can be taken away from the spirit of a natural man is to be born again. To be born again is not to start going to church, neither is it to be serious with God. You are not born again because you were born of Christian parents. To be born again is to be regenerated, to be born of God himself, and to receive his life and nature of God into your spirit. Something literary changes in your spirit when you got born again. To be born again is to have your human life supplanted by the life of God. If you are born again, you are no longer a human being but a god. To be human means to be subject to death, decay, sickness, suffering and poverty. When you are born again, you are born of God and therefore received his nature into you.

You became righteous, holy, sanctified, justified, accepted, and many more just because you are born of God. Human beings give birth to humans, and God gives birth to gods. After being born again, your nature of sin would be replaced by the nature of righteousness. With the nature of righteousness, you can do right; you can stand upright before God and be awakened to the fatherhood of God in your life.

II. The Act Of Sin

Sin is a nature in a man's spirit. It's the nature of sin that causes a man to sin. The act of sin, therefore, is the outward expression of the inner sin nature. Doing something wrong is the outward expression of what is inside. A man who is not born again remains a sinner whether he does something wrong or not. A sinner may choose not to outwardly express what is inside him, but mind you, it's in there. Just like a Christian who inherited the nature of love may also choose not to walk in love, but it's inside him, and anytime he wants to walk in love, he can.

God's problem with the sinners is not necessarily the evil things they do. Many unbelievers don't do terrible things like some Christians even do, but God still has a problem with the sinner because of his nature. People get deceived by thinking most unbelievers are better than some Christians. Such a thought is blasphemy against God. The worst Christian is still far better than the best unbeliever. The believer and the unbeliever have nothing in common and cannot be compared.

Jesus never sinned because he was not born with the nature of sin like any other person. Jesus is the only person born without the nature of sin. Jesus must be born of a virgin without the aid of a man (Joseph) to escape the sin nature from Adam. When a child is conceived, the child's life comes from the father, and the woman gives the seed a body. The Adamic sin nature is stored and transferred through the sperm of a man. Now that Jesus was born without the aid of a man, he was born without the nature of sin.

Jesus never sinned, not because he never did anything we might consider wrong, but those things could not be accounted as sin without the nature of sin. It's the same for a Christian today. A Christian is born of God and has the nature of righteousness, therefore, cannot sin. This is not a joke. If you believe a Christian can still sin, then that Christian should get ready to go to hell because anybody who sins must go to hell. You might ask, "What about all the wrong things a Christian does?" Well, there is a difference between wrongdoing and sin. A Christian does do wrong things but cannot sin. You can sin without doing anything wrong, and you can also do something wrong without sinning.

1 John 3:9 Whoever has been born of God does not sin, for His seed remains in him; and he cannot sin, because he has been born of God.

If you read the above verse with a religious mind, you will only end up confused. Many bible translators don't know what to do with that verse. It blows their mind to see such a thing in the bible. They tried to find several ways to nicely translate it to sound better, but the verse is exactly the way you see it above. He who is born of God cannot sin. If a Christian continues to sin after all Jesus came to do, then his coming is in vain. Get a detailed teaching on the concept of sin and live a glorious life for yourself and Jesus.

You need to understand what the New Testament

made of a Christian. In the New Testament, sin is no longer taking anybody to hell. What is taking a man to hell is unbelief. Men go to hell because they refuse to believe and accept what Jesus came to do for them. The finished work of Jesus brought us power over sin. No Christian is supposed to find himself struggling with sin.

Romans 6:14 For sin shall not have dominion over you: for ye are not under the law, but under grace.

You are free from sin; you can live a sin-free life; you just don't know it. If you are struggling with sin, it's because you didn't know you have power over sin. Now that you know it, you can walk out of any sin. Exercise the power given to you over sin and be free.

Chapter Seven

Kinds of Sin

Sin can also be looked at from three other angles. These are sources through which sin gets into a man's life. I know very well that the concept of sin is a subject many Christians will never understand because they have created their own sins and are living in the bondage of them. Man only sins against God, and therefore God is the best person to decide what sin is. As humans we wrong one another but sin against God. Let's look at some other intriguing concepts of sin.

Inherited Sin

The first kind or source of sin is inherited sin. This is the primary source of sin in a man's life. Every man primarily became a sinner because they inherited sin. This sinful nature was inherited from Adam, and I explained how in the above chapters. The moment a man is born into the world, he is born a sinner not because he did or didn't do anything; it's a nature inherited.

Psalms 51:5 Behold, I was brought forth in iniquity, And in sin, my mother conceived me.

That's why it's inaccurate to think you are righteous because you don't do anything wrong. Yes, you don't do wrong things but you inherited sin. That is why Jesus didn't specify who should be born again. Everybody must be born again and be very sure he is truly regenerated. Jesus said in ***John 3:7 Marvel not that I said unto thee, Ye <u>must</u> be born again.*** He didn't say you should consider being born again, but you must. It's a necessity because the first birth from your parents came with the nature of sin. The nature you need to be in the kingdom of God is the nature of righteousness which comes from another birth. A man becomes a sinner due to the sin he inherits from his grandfather Adam.

Imputed Sin

The second kind of sin is imputed sin. This is the kind of sin or impact of sin that affects a person due to the transgression of a relative (parent, a family member, a leader, nation). Imputed sin is when you suffer consequences from a sin committed by a related person. This has to do with your association with the transgressor. This type of sin is also not necessarily committed by the person who suffers the consequences but rather by a person or group of people related to him. Imputed sin is also one of the sins that affected every human being from the transgression of Adam.

Every man born into this world would suffer some form of difficulty due to Adam's transgression. If not for Adam's disobedience, the world wouldn't have been as it is today. It would have been a paradise for all men. But from Adam's transgression, every man has something to suffer one way or the other; sickness, poverty, rejection, disappointment, death, tiredness, etc. Besides imputed sin from Adam, there are so many other imputed sins that can affect a man. Let me outline a few.

Family-imputed sin: it's a sin affecting a person due to a transgression from a family member. Transgression here is not necessarily a sin. Family members may suffer physical or spiritual consequences as a result of the way of life of the past family members. The new generation may suffer consequences such as poverty, spiritual attacks, bad family names, rejections etc. as a result of idol worship or a crime committed by a family member. For example, it may be hard for some family members to find a partner because of a bad family history. Nobody will be willing to marry from such a family because of the bad family history a member left behind.

The current members are not the ones who committed those crimes, but they are the ones suffering the consequences. Some other families are poor because their great-grandfathers didn't study hard in school. All the wealthy families we have today were brought about by one person who worked hard and got great opportunities to change the family. How you are living your life today will also leave something behind for your children to enjoy or to suffer.

Let me show you one perfect example in the Bible about imputed sin. In Mathew chapter 23, Jesus taught the multitude and his disciples about the character of the Scribes and the Pharisees. Teaching them, he admonishes them to do everything these religious leaders asked them to do because they sit in Moses' seat. In other words, God placed them in authority, so Jesus admonished them to obey them even though they don't do the things they asked others to do. Take your Bible and read the whole of Mathew 23 for a better understanding.

As the teaching went on, Jesus began to pronounce woes of punishment, judgment, and condemnation that awaited these religious leaders concerning the aspects they serve as stumbling blocks *(Mathew 23:13-29)*. It even gets worse from verse 29. Let me quote from verse 29 to the end and show you something.

Mathew 23:29-36 "Woe to you, scribes and Pharisees, hypocrites! Because you build the tombs of the prophets and adorn the monuments of the righteous, ³⁰ and <u>say, 'If we had lived in the days of our fathers</u>, we would not have been partakers with them in the blood of the prophets.'

³¹"Therefore <u>you are witnesses against yourselves that you are sons of those who murdered the prophets.</u> ³² Fill up, then, the measure of your fathers' guilt. ³³ Serpents, brood of vipers! How can you escape the condemnation of hell? ³⁴ Therefore, indeed, I send you prophets, wise men, and scribes: some of them you will kill and crucify, and some of them you will scourge in your synagogues and persecute from city to city, ³⁵ <u>that on you may come all the righteous blood shed on the earth, from the blood of righteous Abel to the blood of Zechariah, son of Berechiah, whom you murdered between the temple and the altar. ³⁶ Assuredly, I say to you,</u>

Look at the underlined phrases very well. These Scribes and Pharisees, trying to defend themselves, said, "Well, if they were to be in the day of their forefathers, they wouldn't have partaken in the killing of the prophets" Jesus said "Now that they called those who killed the prophets their fathers, they have confirmed their association with them and therefore all their punishments will come on them. How is that possible? Imputed sin by association. These Scribes and Pharisees associated themselves with their forefathers who killed the prophets sent to them many years ago by calling them fathers.

Now Jesus said because they associated themselves with them, they qualified to partake in their damnation. This new generation will pay for the sins of all the righteous men ever killed from Abel; the son of Adam to the last prophet before Jesus. What a punishment! This portion of the Bible is the greatest judgment and condemnation in the Bible. This current generation was not the one who killed the prophets, but they are going to suffer imputed sin because of association. That should tell you how important your associations are. You can read the rest of Mathew 23:37-39 into chapter 24:1. Jesus lamented over Jerusalem and departed from the temple. That was how Israel was rejected by God for 2000 with several destructive events happening to them.

Just look at the great punishment they brought upon themselves by association. People are sick, suffering, in prison, and even dead today not because of anything they did but the people they associated themselves with. As far as you associate yourself with the sinner, you will suffer imputed sin. Same way, when you associate yourself with godly men, you enjoy imputed righteousness. Imputed sin and imputed righteousness happen as a result of association.

National imputed sin: These are consequences citizens of a country suffer due to bad decisions or actions from their leaders. When leaders make bad decisions, the citizens suffer the consequences. That is why God said to pray for our leaders. Whether you like them or not, pray for them because their decisions affect you.

1 Timothy 2:1-2 NKJV I exhort therefore, that, first of all, supplications, prayers, intercessions, and giving of thanks, be made for all men; 2 For kings, and for all that are in authority; that we may lead a quiet and peaceable life in all godliness and honesty.

Citizens of many countries are victims of national imputed sin. There are sufferings everywhere, not because things can't be done right in that country but because of bad leadership. Most of our national leaders are being used by demonic forces to do things or make policies that will make life difficult for them citizens. You may not be the one making those bad decisions, but you still have to suffer the hardship. You owe your leaders prayers. You need to pray for any form of leadership above you, for them to make sound decisions for the betterment of your life.

Make it a habit to pray for your country in particular. That's where you hail from and have an association with the leaders of that country. How do you get yourself under or out of these imputed sins? The only way to escape these imputed sins is to be born again. When you give your life to Christ, you will have new authority and associations over your life. Whatever affects Christ affects you. Anytime you pledge an alliance with a thing or someone, you will suffer or enjoy whatever affects them. That's why you need to pledge your alliance with Christ and enjoy the life and glory he has to give his people. The primary imputed sin is from Adam to all humans, but your alliance with Christ can make a big difference for you.

Personal Sin

The third kind of sin is Personal sin. This is the kind of sin committed by an individual. Personal sin is the consequences you suffer as a result of the kind of life you are living. If you do evil things, it comes with consequences immediately or later. Live your life right so you don't bring any pain and suffering upon yourself. Remember, your life today is going to leave something for the generation after you to enjoy or to suffer. Live right!

Have you realised that before a person starts sinning, he has two kinds of sin already affecting him; inherited and imputed sin? This is the reason he must give his life to Christ. It's not about you not doing anything evil; it's about your nature. No matter how good a person may be, he must still give his life to Christ.

Chapter Eight
Kinds of Righteousness

We just discussed three kinds of sin—the sources from which one can acquire sin in his life. We also have the same concept of righteousness. Righteousness comes from three sources: inherited righteousness, imputed righteousness, and personal righteousness. Let's dive into the details.

Inherited Righteousness

Inherited righteousness is the righteousness we inherited from Christ when we were born again. You received the nature of righteousness by virtue of your new birth. Inherited sin comes from Adam, and inherited righteousness comes from Jesus Christ. Righteousness is the nature every Christian is born with.

2 Corinthians 5:21 For he hath made him to be sin for us, who knew no sin; that we might be made the righteousness of God in him.

Jesus was made sin so we can be righteous, which has happened already. No Christian should struggle to be righteous because you are righteous already. The nature of sin causes the sinner to sin, and the nature of righteousness causes the Christian to do right. You received that nature when you were born again, and nothing can change that nature. It's a free gift from God the Father to you. You don't need to do anything to become righteous. Just receive the free gift and walk in the light of it.

Romans 5:17 For if by one man's offense death reigned by one, much more those who receive abundance of grace and <u>the gift of righteousness</u> shall reign in life by One, Jesus Christ.

Did you see that? It's those who received the gift of righteousness that will reign, not those who are trying to be righteous. Just carry the consciousness of your righteousness, and don't let anything deceive you otherwise. You were born with it in Christ Jesus.

1 Corinthians 1:30 But of him are ye in Christ Jesus, who of God is made unto us wisdom, and righteousness, and sanctification, and redemption: that, according as it is written, He that glorieth, let him glory in the Lord.

Christ is made unto you righteousness. Hallelujah! Now that you are righteous, you will always be righteous. You can't grow in righteousness. In other words, you can't be more or less righteous than you are now. Just like you can't be more female or more male than you are now. Your inherited righteousness came from Christ, and its quality is dependent on his righteousness. With this nature of righteousness, you can do right and approach God the Father always without a sense of guilt.

Imputed Righteousness

Imputed righteousness is the righteousness or the

blessings you enjoy due to your association with a righteous man. Just as every man suffered imputed sin from Adam, so does every Christian also enjoy imputed righteousness from Christ Jesus. What a blessing!

Galatians 3:14 NLT Through Christ Jesus, God has blessed the Gentiles with the same blessing he promised to Abraham, so that we who are believers might receive the promised Holy Spirit through faith.

Ephesians 1:3 Blessed be the God and Father of our Lord Jesus Christ, who hath blessed us with all spiritual blessings in heavenly places in Christ,

Can you see the blessings and the promises we received due to our association with Christ? All of God's blessings are in Christ Jesus, and our association qualifies us to enjoy those blessings. You remember we learned that Imputed sin comes from association, and so is imputed righteousness. Imputed righteousness can also come from a relative. Those whose forefathers lived righteous lives are enjoying their blessings today. Many people are enjoying God's blessings today because of a relative who walked with God. God's hands, mercy, and kindness are on some families and nations today because they had people who walked in righteousness. The nation of Israel is as mighty with God's hand mightily upon it because of their great fathers who had a covenant with God. That is imputed righteousness. To enjoy imputed righteousness, you have to associate yourself with righteous people. If you associate yourself with sinners, you suffer their punishment.

Personal Righteousness

This is the righteous fruits you produce as you manifest the righteousness of God. Personal righteousness is the blessings you enjoy as you walk in God's righteousness imparted to you. As you walk with God, his blessings are apportioned to you, and you can also leave this blessing for the generations after you. Make up your mind to walk in righteousness, and surely, you will have a great personal righteousness.

New Testament Concept Of Sin And Righteousness

The concept of sin and righteousness under the New Testament or Covenant is one of the controversial subjects in Christianity today. I know of the numerous and diverting teachings regarding sin making it hard for many young Christians to understand the concept fully. When you listen carefully and pay attention to the details of every teaching, you will know the right ones from the wrong ones.

One of the main purposes of the coming of Jesus is to deal with sin and its effects. He didn't come to die for us to keep sinning and receiving forgiveness. He came to completely eliminate sin. In other words, he came to completely remove sin from us. If he was successful in his mission, we ought to be people free from sin, except he was not successful.

His death dealt with sin, defeated sin, paralysed sin, and rendered sin powerless over us. Not just that, at our new birth, he gave us a nature that made us superior to sin and its effects, which is the nature of righteousness. John understanding this boldly said in *1 John 3:9 Whosoever is born of God doth not commit sin; for his seed remaineth in him: and he cannot sin, because he is born of God.* That should tell you who a Christian is.

This book cannot fully discuss the whole concept of sin. Think about these questions: who is a Christian? When does he sin? What does he do to sin? What is sin? Who do we sin against? When a Christian sin, what must he do? By the time you finish reading this book, I know you will get answers to all these questions.

What was sin under the Old Testament is different from what sin is under the New Testament. Let me use righteousness to explain it. The measuring standard of sin is righteousness. The Old Testament people could become righteous when they obeyed the Laws and the commandments of Moses. Therefore, they will sin when they can't meet that righteousness by disobeying the Laws and the commandments of Moses. *1 John 3:4-5 Whosoever committeth sin transgresseth also the law: <u>for sin is the transgression of the law.</u>*

I hope you noticed he didn't say, "Sin is the transgression of **a law**," but of **the law**. That is talking about the law of Moses. So, they sinned when they broke the law. The New Testament people became righteous by expressing their faith in Jesus Christ, by which they received a new birth, which comes with the nature of righteousness. The New Testament saint was born with the nature of righteousness. We have been given no law and commandments to obey. I know of the commandment to love one another, but love is our nature. The New Testament saint sins by not walking in faith.

Romans 14:23 And he that doubteth is damned if he eat, because he eateth not of faith: <u>for whatsoever is not of faith is sin.</u>

Interestingly, in the New Testament, sin is personal and optional. In other words, what I may do to sin, you may do the same thing, and it may not be sin. You sin according to the personal instructions given to you by God, and everyone's instructions are not the same even though we might have some common instructions. Specific instructions are given to everyone patterning their walk with God. That is the main reason why God did not give us the power to judge. Sometimes, God is behind the very things someone is doing that you think is wrong. You see, the concept is not the same in both testaments. The old law was written on tablets, the New law is written in our hearts. Read more on the optionality of sin on page 118.

Chapter Nine

Regeneration of the Christian

This chapter introduces you to what it means to be born again. We will discuss how a man can be recreated, the principles and the results of being born again.

From the previous chapters, we looked at man's creation and fall. From the fall, we defined sin as taking authority into your hands to define good and evil instead of God's definition of good and evil. We also discussed how every man inherited that authority from Adam by birth and therefore became a sinner. Jesus came for the salvation of the sinner. His main reason for coming was to completely save man from sin and its effects and give man the power over sin through righteousness.

His birth, death and resurrection have accomplished something the human mind cannot comprehend. He made it possible for the sinner to be recreated and made righteous; that's the greatest miracle in human history. Let's look at how a man becomes born again.

The Concept Of Being Born Again

A Christian is not an ordinary person; a Christian is a person who is born again. Born again here, I mean regenerated or recreated; that means a person who is born of God. To be born again, you have to be born from the realms of the spirit, unlike your first birth, which is from the physical realm. It doesn't mean to start going to church or to stop doing all the bad things you were doing and start doing the right things. Again, it doesn't mean to be serious with God or to turn a new leaf in life. To be born again means to be recreated by the Word of God under the urgency of the Holy Spirit. It's the best thing that can ever happen to a man. It's to consciously accept the Lordship of Jesus Christ over your life and live for him. When that happens, your human life will be supplanted with the life of God. To be born again is far more than praying the sinner's prayer. You can pray the sinner's prayer several times and still won't be born again.

To be born again is to receive a new spirit of righteousness to replace your old spirit of sin. In other words, your spirit, which is associated with Adam's is completely removed, and a brand-new spirit of righteousness is given to you. The new regenerated spirit comes with a completely new life full of limitless possibilities. With this new spirit, you can stand upright with God. To be born again is the awakening to the fatherhood of God over your life.

The Principle Of Being Born Again

The Bible shows us how a person can be born again. It's one of the simplest but most powerful principle ever revealed to men. Let's look at the principle and how it works.

Romans 10:9 That if thou shalt confess with thy mouth the Lord Jesus, and shalt believe in thine heart that God hath raised him from the dead, thou shalt be saved.

Salvation is initiated by you believing the gospel in your heart. Your heart here refers to your spirit. You believe spiritual things with your spirit and not your mind. You can't believe spiritual things with your mind; they won't make sense because they are not meant to make sense. When you listen to the Word of God, say "yes!" to it, agree with it and act on it. Everybody can believe; those who say they can't believe don't want to believe, not because they can't.

For you to be born again, what are you supposed to believe? You need to believe that *Jesus is the Son of God, he came to this world to die for your sins and God raised him back to life, and he is alive today and will one day very soon return to rule this world as a king.* You may say "I haven't seen him, how do I believe?" You haven't seen your intestines, but you believe they are there. Just accept anything you are told about Jesus for now and start your Christian journey. Start going to church to learn about him. Enter into a relationship with him, and he will soon become so real to you.

After you believe, you have to confess what you believe. You need to utter what you believe. It's not enough to believe; you must publicly declare, confess, profess, and demonstrate what you believe. Believing alone is not enough because the Bible says even demons believe and tremble (James 2:19). If you believe and don't take any action, your belief won't be any different from the demons. Demons believe but can't confess. They believe but can't act on what they believe because they rebel against God. There is nothing as evil as not believing in God. That is a sin even Satan won't commit. Satan believes in God.

James 2:19 Thou believest that there is one God; thou doest well: the devils also believe, and tremble.

Roman 10:9 told us what to confess. Interestingly, it's not our sins. Thanks be to God for that. He says to confess the Lordship of Jesus Christ by declaring that he was raised from the dead. That verse never asked anybody to confess his sins. You don't get born again by confessing your sins because you can't confess your sins. Man doesn't have enough knowledge about sin to confess them. The Bible says that when you receive the gospel preached to you and believe it, confess it, and you will be saved.

Why Must We Confess The Resurrection?

When Jesus died, the religious and political leaders were really happy. They met together to celebrate his death. While celebrating, someone raised a concern. He said, "I quite remember when Jesus was alive, he said he would die and return to life on the third day. For our good, let's send soldiers to go and guard the tomb; if God raises him back to life, they can kill him again" They did as the guy suggested. They assigned many soldiers and spread themselves all over the garden, waiting for him to rise from the dead.

Mathew 27:62-66 Now the next day, that followed the day of the preparation, the chief priests and Pharisees came together unto Pilate, [63] Saying, Sir, we remember that that deceiver said, while he was yet alive, After three days I will rise again. [64] Command therefore that the sepulchre be made sure until the third day, lest his disciples come by night, and steal him away, and say unto the people, He is risen from the dead: so the last error shall be worse than the first. [65] Pilate said unto them, Ye have a watch: go your way, make it as sure as ye can. [66] So they went, and made the sepulchre sure, sealing the stone, and setting a watch.

On the third day, an angel of the Lord came to roll the stone from the tomb; his brightness and presence were so great that the soldiers couldn't stand it. They had to run for their lives. Running for their lives, they remember they were assigned by their leaders, so, they decided to go to the city to report what happened and their experiences to the leaders. They confirmed to the leaders that Jesus was indeed risen from the dead and is alive. The religious leaders thought this would be a big defeat and that something must be done immediately. So, the Bible says they had a meeting. From the meeting, they decided to give the soldiers a large sum of money to go into the city and tell as many as they could that Jesus had not risen from the dead, but his disciples came by night and stole his body away. The leaders promised to secure them in case the governor heard about the resurrection.

The soldiers took the money and did as they were commanded. They went and spread the lie throughout the cities. The Bible says this lie remains in Israel till today. For this reason, the Jews don't believe in the resurrection of Jesus. This is why the Jews are not Christians because Christianity started from the resurrection of Jesus and not his death.

Mathew 28:11-14 Now when they were going, behold, some of the watch came into the city, and shewed unto the chief priests all the things that were done. [12] And when they were assembled with the elders, and had taken counsel, they gave large money unto the soldiers, [13] Saying, Say ye, His disciples came by night, and stole him away while we slept. [14] And if this come to the governor's ears, we will persuade him, and secure you. [15] So they took the money, and did as they were taught: and this saying is commonly reported among the Jews until this day.

When the above incident happened, God passed it through law that for anybody to be saved, he must believe and declare that He (almighty God) raised His Son Jesus from the dead as he promised. If you declare it and believe it, then you will be saved. Look at that verse again.

Romans 10:9 That if thou shalt confess with thy mouth the Lord Jesus, and shalt believe in thine heart that God hath raised him from the dead, thou shalt be saved.

That is the principle of being born again. Let's look at the next verse, which explains how the principle works.

Romans 10:10 For with the heart man believeth unto righteousness, and with the mouth confession is made unto salvation.

It says that when you believe with your heart (spirit), you believe unto righteousness. That means your believing makes you upright with God. When you hear the Word of God and believe it in your heart, the Word immediately prepares your heart and makes you ready to be regenerated (recreated, born again). That is the power of the Word of God. When the Word comes into contact with your spirit, the Word then makes the sinner upright with God and prepares him to be born again. The moment the sinner opens his mouth and declares the Lordship of Jesus, he is immediately regenerated in the spirit *... and with the mouth confession is made unto salvation (Romans 10:10).*

Confession must always follow your beliefs. Confession here is not necessarily with your mouth; it's the confession of your heart. You can actually be born again without praying the sinner's prayer aloud. The apostles got born again when the Holy Spirit came on them. They didn't pray any sinner's prayer. Most of us weren't born again when we prayed the sinner's prayer, but it happened later when we started going to church, and our spirits opened to the Word of God. Don't play games with your salvation. Make sure you genuinely give your life to Christ and start walking in the Spirit.

Make sure you have enough evidence within you that you are born again; don't just assume you are born again and be hoping to go to heaven one day. Get the assurance in you and make sure the Holy Spirit is indeed working in you. If you want to know your level as a Christian, find out how many of the fruits of the spirit have you developed. Those fruits can be found in Galatians 5:22-23. In case you are not born again too, turn to the back of this book and pray the prayer of salvation and you will be saved.

Chapter Ten
Seven Facts of a Christian

The most extraordinary being on earth today is the Christian. If you think the human body is the most complex machine, the Christian is even more complex. In this chapter, we will look at some amazing realities of who a Christian is. That will introduce us to what God has made of a mortal man.

1. A Christian Is A New Creation

As we discussed, when you are born again, your old spirit from your parents, which is associated with the sin of Adam, is taken out of you, and a new spirit is given to you. You are born with a brand-new spirit from God. This new spirit is a brand-new spirit that never existed before and therefore has no past. Your "past life" went away with your old spirit. That is one of the reasons why Christians won't face judgment or condemnation for Adam's transgression. You are a new species, a new breed, from a special class with no earthly origin. You are a god born of God himself. Your parents cannot give birth to such a species, it's only God that can do that. Hallelujah!

If you are born again, don't allow anybody to judge you with your past life, no matter how terrible it was. Those bad things you did are not affecting you now. But it's your responsibility to clear your conscience with the Word of God. That is what God meant in **_Romans 12:2 And be not conformed to this world: but be ye transformed by the renewing of your mind,_** ... Can you see it's your responsibility to renew your mind? When we sin, we sin against God and not man. If God has no problem with you, no man, not even yourself, has the right to judge you with your past life. Feel free to serve God, and don't feel guilty about your past life, for God is not holding them against you.

Some people can't forget their past because of the scars of consequences they carry on their bodies or the way it's impacting their lives today. Yes, that's why God warned us to live an upright life. God doesn't want you to do wrong things, not because he can't forgive you but because of the consequences you might face due to those wrong things. For example, if a prisoner repents and gives his life to Christ in prison, God will accept him and forgive him of any sin, including the murder that took him to jail, but he may have to stay in prison until his days are fulfilled. Do you see that? God may forgive you your sins but you may have to pay certain prices not as punishment from God.

When you gave your life to Christ, it was your spirit that was recreated. Nothing might change on the outside, but your spirit is brand-new. Have that consciousness that you are a new creation, a brand-new man, and serve God with that consciousness. Satan loves to use people's past lives against them to hold them in bondage and make them ineffective

Christians. Don't allow that to happen to you. Be conscious of who God has made you. You are his loved child, his first and the best. God loves you as though there is no other person on earth. He is mindful of you more than you can ever be of yourself.

2. A Christian Is Born Of God

As you receive the gospel, believe it, and confess the Lordship of Jesus, God the Father regenerated you, by the Word of God under the urgency of the Holy Spirit. This new birth is from God himself. You became a child of God because you were born of him. Your first birth was from your parents, that's why you were affected by the Adamic sin. Your new birth is from God himself, so you were born righteous. When a dog gives birth, the offspring will be a dog. When God give birth, the offspring will be a god. You are a god because you are born of God.

Psalm 82:5-7 They know not, neither will they

understand; they walk on in darkness: all the foundations of the earth are out of course. ⁶ <u>I have said, Ye are gods;</u> and all of you are children of the most High. ⁷ <u>But ye shall die like men,</u> and fall like one of the princes.

Have you seen the underlined statement? God declared you to be a god. Verse 7 says you will die like a man if you don't know or understand it. If he says your lack of knowledge will cause you to die like a man, that means you were not a man (human being). Read those verses again. They are verses that need maximum attention. If you are not well convinced, look at the verses below.

John 1:11-13 (KJV) He came unto his own, and his own received him not. ¹² But as many as received him, to them gave he power to become the sons of God, even to them that believe on his name: ¹³ Which were born, not of blood, nor of the will of the flesh, nor of the will of man, but of God.

John 1:11-13 (NIV) He came to that which was his own, but his own did not receive him. ¹² <u>Yet to</u>

<u>*all who did receive him*</u>*, to* <u>*those who believed in his name*</u>*, he gave the right to become children of God *[13]* children born not of natural descent, nor of human decision or a husband's will,* <u>*but born of God.*</u>

Who are the people born of God? The Jews who believed in him when he walked the surface of this earth. The apostles, disciples, Nicodemus, and any other person who received him even though the Jews rejected him. That is the first group born of God. The second group is those who believe his name; that's you and I. The Bible says these two groups were born of God. The consciousness of being born of God can make a big difference in your life. The president's son has a mentality, a child of God should also have a mentality, the mentality of being born of God.

3. A Christian Is Born With The Nature Of God

Nature is something that only comes by birth. For example, you are a guy or lady by nature. The nature of the natural man is wickedness, hatred, jealousy, betrayal, envy, backbiting, disappointment, etc. (Galatians5:19-21). The natural man is born with these evil virtues. Now that we are born of God, we are born with a new nature from God. The nature of righteousness, kindness, mercy, forgiveness, patience, love, goodness etc (Galatians 5:22-23). Love is not the nature of men. The natural man cannot love. Humans can only love with "human love", and human love is dangerous. The natural man only loves when there are benefits. What makes human love dangerous is that it demands more in return than it gives, and when the demand is not met, it hurts or damages you.

But a Christian can genuinely love with the love of God if he wants to. You might say, "But I know many Christians who are not walking in love" Well, just like a lady can choose to dress and act like a guy even though she is a lady, so can a Christian also decide not to walk in love even though he could. The same for righteousness; every Christian was born righteous. Righteousness is the nature of God given to you. Every Christian can walk in righteousness; a Christian may also decide not to, even though they could. Many Christians are waiting to be righteous before they walk in righteousness; the truth is you were born righteous. Righteousness is not a lifestyle. It's not your right living that makes you righteous but your nature of righteousness that gives you the ability to live right.

The same applies to forgiveness. You have the ability to forgive. If you are still finding it difficult to forgive others as a Christian, it's just because you made up your mind not to forgive. Don't pray to God to give you patience. You have it already; walk in it. You have all the natures of God in you, study about them and walk in the fullness of God. Examples of the nature of God are righteousness, holiness, kindness, patience, love, endurance, faithfulness, forgiveness, etc. Read Galatians 5:22-23 for more.

These gifts are not things you assume you have; you have them. When the Holy Spirit came into you, he brought God into you. How glorious it feels to think about the fact that you have the nature of God and can love, forgive, have mercy, be kind, and be holy, just like God.

4. A Christian Is Saved From The Judgement And Condemnation Of God

Many Christians still fear to hear of the soon-coming Jesus Christ. They can't imagine what will happen next after he comes. Jesus is not coming to judge and condemn the Christians. That will only happen to the unbeliever. You have been saved from that judgment. All Christians know they have been saved, but most of us don't know exactly what we were saved from, and therefore we are still afraid of the same things we were saved from. A Christian is saved from the wrath, judgment and condemnation of God. Jesus was already judged, punished, and condemned to hell on your behalf to save us from eternal judgment. No Christian will be judged to be condemned.

The judgment day is in two categories. The first one has to do with only Christians and Christ. No unbeliever will be allowed to that judgment; it's the judgment for reward. It's the moment when all Christians will be called forward one by one to be celebrated and appreciated by Jesus for their contribution towards the Kingdom of God while on earth. It's that moment when all your work will be quantified, and you will be rewarded.

The judgment day will be the most exciting day in the life of every Christian. Even those who won't receive any reward will be happy to the full. The other category is the judgment of the unbelievers. They are the ones to face the terrible wrath of God for not believing his Son, Jesus Christ. They are the ones God will pour his anger and condemnation on.

God knew nobody could face that judgment, so he made provision for all men to be saved. Hallelujah! Never be afraid of the judgment day or the coming of Christ again. It's rather a day you should look forward to.

Salvation By Grace

Our salvation came by grace. It means you didn't do anything to qualify for it. Jesus is your qualification. The Old Testament people had to obey laws and commandments to be saved. They needed to work for their salvation. For those of us in the New Testament, Jesus did all the works for us. Your performance as a Christian is based on the performance of Jesus. All you need is to believe in all he did for you and express your faith in him and you will be saved. It's called salvation by faith.

Assurance Of Salvation

Have you ever wondered if you are saved? Have you ever wondered if all these things about Christianity are really true? Did God really mean what he said in His Word? You have every right to ask those questions because you want to be sure if you believe the right stuff. But if you have been born again for some time, you should have full assurance of your salvation by now. Let us examine the top two assurances of your salvation.

I. The Word Of God.

The word of God is your first assurance. Satan makes God's children feel they are not saved or have to work hard to be saved. But our faith in the Word of God assures us that we are saved. Let's examine that verse in Romans chapter 10 again.

That <u>if thou shalt confess</u> with thy mouth the Lord Jesus, <u>and shalt believe in thine heart</u> that God hath raised him from the dead, <u>thou shalt be saved</u>.

By using the word "if" means there is a condition.

Let's look at the condition. ***If you shall confess with your mouth and shall believe in your heart,*** the result of that condition is salvation. That means every Christian must meet that condition for their salvation. That condition is also your assurance of salvation. God says if I confess and believe, I will be saved. I have confessed, I have believed, and therefore I am saved. I have met the condition for salvation and therefore, I am saved. If only you met that condition, then you are fully saved. All you need to do now is to walk in the consciousness of your salvation.

Ii. The Witness Of The Holy Spirit

Romans 8:16 The Spirit himself testifies with our spirit that we are God's children.

The Holy Spirit bears witness with your spirit that you are a child of God. That is why the Holy Spirit was given to help you with your Christian journey. He does the inner witness. We have something inside us we can't explain with our mouths, and we know we have received something when we gave our lives to God. Whenever there is doubt in your heart, look inside you. We do everything we do because we know what we believe is true. We belong to a kingdom that is so real to us, and nothing can convince us otherwise. Those who were killed for their faith died happily because they knew they were dying for a righteous course. There is just that inner witness inside us we can't help. It's the witness of the Holy Spirit.

Those are the two assurances you should hold on to as a Christian. The Word of God and the witness of the Holy Spirit. Your salvation is well secured. God is never going to change his mind about you. He meant everything he said in His Word about your salvation.

5. Sins Remitted And Forgiveness Available For The Christian.

The subject of remission and forgiveness is very important for every Christian to understand. There is a big difference between the remission of sin and the forgiveness of sin. Knowing the difference will help you understand the subject of sin well.

Remission of sin is the complete removal or blotting away of sin and its effects on a man's life. This is when sins are forgiven and forgotten as though they were never committed. When sins are remitted, no record can be found anywhere; not even God can remember. When a sinner is saved, he receives remission of sin. The sinner doesn't need forgiveness of sin; he needs remission of sin. Remission of sin was not possible in the Old Testament. Their sins could not be completely removed but were only covered for a year, and there is a remembrance again. Jesus made remission possible for us.

Luke 24:46-47 And said unto them, Thus it is

written, and thus it behoved Christ to suffer, and to rise from the dead the third day: [47] And that <u>repentance and remission</u> of sins should be preached in his name among all nations, beginning at Jerusalem.

A sinner cannot receive forgiveness of sin if his sins are not first remitted. God is not that wicked to be unforgiving to the whole world. He is not happy to see billions of people unsaved. He can forgive every man's sin in a split second which is actually in his power to do. But he can't forgive because the sinner first needs remission of sin, and the decision for that is in the hands of the sinner. All the sinner needs is to accept the Lordship of Jesus and his sins will be remitted. When you do something wrong after remission, then can your wrongdoings be forgiven by God. The decision for sin to be remitted is in the hands of the sinner, and then God can have the power to forgive him when he does something wrong.

There is also a difference between sinning and

doing something wrong. You can sin without doing anything wrong and do something wrong without sinning. Sin has been completely dealt with and removed from the life of the Christian. Sin is not supposed to be a problem for any Christian. Sin is not taking anybody to hell anymore. What takes a man to hell today is not sin but rather unbelief. People go to hell today because they didn't believe in Jesus and haven't accepted his Lordship. They don't believe he went to hell on their behalf, so they have to go to hell for themselves. If you are already born again, your sins are already remitted, and when you do something wrong, ask God for forgiveness, and he will forgive you right away.

6. *To Sin Is A Choice For The Christian*

Religiosity is making many Christians ineffective in their dealing with God. I want to discuss a subject that will blow the mind of some and bless others. A Christian is a mystery that the human mind can't understand. A Christian born of God cannot sin.

Don't forget we Christians were not restored to the nature Adam had before his fall. If we were restored to that nature, what made Adam fall would make us fall again. We are a completely new species. A Christian belongs to God's class of life. The life we were born with is incompatible with sin, disease, and poverty; every Christian must understand that.

1 John 3:9 Whoever has been born of God does not sin, for His seed remains in him; and he cannot sin, because he has been born of God.

The verse above is only accurate in the King James Version. All other translations viewed the verse religiously. They can't believe such a thing could be in the Bible. So, they try to translate it into something appealing to the human mind. The verse is exactly what you read. Because of the seed of God in us, we cannot sin. Many Christians don't even know what sin is; they don't even know exactly what they have to do to sin. A Christian is born with the seed of the Word of God. Our very nature is the Word, and this nature cannot sin. The verse says the seed remains in us. In case you are not well convinced, look at another verse below.

1 John 2: 1 <u>My little children,</u> these things write I unto you, <u>that you sin not.</u> And <u>if any man sin,</u> we have an advocate with the Father, Jesus Christ the righteous:

1 John chapter 2 is a no-go place for religious people. They don't know what to make of those verses. In that chapter, John addressed three categories of people; the little children, the young men and the fathers. He communicated a unique message to each group according to their level of dealing with God. He addressed the little children first.

1 John 2: 1 <u>My little children,</u> these things write I unto you, <u>that you sin not.</u> And <u>if any man sin,</u> we have an advocate with the Father, Jesus Christ the righteous:

Little children are the spiritually immature Christians. Those who don't know much about the Word of God. This is not only those who just gave their lives to Christ but anybody who isn't exposed to the teachings of God's Word. Little children are the ones who have problems with sin, so John addressing them, addressed them in that light. But look at what he told them even as little children. Read the verse above again. He told them not to sin. That means it's possible not to sin. If it's not possible, he wouldn't have asked them to. He took them further since they are little children who may sometimes go out of range. John said, "If any of them sin, we have an advocate with the Father who will take care of it" Have you noticed John didn't say "when any man sins" but "if any man sins" "If" is a conditional word, it means it's not compulsory. John is saying they shouldn't sin, but in case any of them sin, an advocate will take care of it. Did you notice he didn't say they should ask for forgiveness if they sinned? He said the advocate will take care of it. What a blessing!

It's not compulsory to sin; to sin is optional. You decide to sin, and you can also choose not to sin. That is why it's inappropriate for a prayer leader to lead a church congregation to ask God for forgiveness in church. Sin is personal; when you sin, I might not sin; therefore, when you sin, go ahead and ask God for forgiveness and, likewise, any other person. It's an insult to Jesus to hear a whole congregation begging God for forgiveness of sin. It's a spit on his face. Do you mean to say Jesus died to produce a people still struggling with sin? What then is the essence of his death? It's a shame for the church to do that. Never catch yourself in such a congregation again. It's one of the best ways to render the death of Jesus in vain. We have been given power over sin.

Romans 6:14 For sin shall not have dominion over you: for ye are not under the law, but under grace.

If you are still struggling with sin, exercise the authority you have been given in Jesus over it. Make sure you are exercising dominion over sin as a Christian because that is who Jesus made you.

7. *A Christian Must Feed On The Word Of God*

Your born-again spirit was sourced from the Word of God; therefore, you must feed on the Word of God for your continued existence. Every living thing must remain connected to its source. Plants must remain connected to the soil to continue living; fishes must remain connected to water. Your recreated human spirit must remain connected to the Word of God to continue to live. When you disconnect yourself from the Word, you begin to die.

You must make a conscious effort to feed on the word of God. Study your bible, listen to tapes, attend training programs and conferences, and attend church regularly. When you go to church, pay attention to every aspect of the service. All church services and activities were designed for your spiritual effectiveness and growth. Don't be selective with the services and the activities. Learning the Word of God is your responsibility. No one can do that for you. There are amazing realities you will discover when reading your Bible that you will never hear from any preacher. Studying your bible personally keeps your Christian life in check and removes the guilt of not growing as Satan always does to Christians. Give reverence to the Word of God and live according to the message of the Word, and you will live.

Chapter Eleven

The New You in Christ

Man is a spirit who has a soul and lives in the body. Every human being is primarily a spirit. The real you is your spirit; you are not your body. Let's look at the three aspects of man. Man is a tripartite being, not a trinity. Man has three parts; the spirit, the soul, and the body.

The Spirit

As we learnt from chapter two, man was first created a spirit before being given a body. The original you is your spirit. Your spirit takes all your decisions. With your spirit, you relate with God and the spirit realm. You hear and respond to the Word of God with your spirit. Your spirit is your essence of living.

A person is dead when his spirit leaves his body. Your spirit doesn't die it only leaves the body. Now that you are a spirit, you will live eternally. The difference between the spirit of the believer and the unbeliever is where they are going to spend eternity. Your spirit is mostly referred to in the Word of God as your heart, the inner man or the innermost being. It was the one that got regenerated when you got born again.

The Soul

Your soul is defined as the seat of your mind, will, and emotions. It is the centre for coordinating information. The controlling centre of the soul is the mind; that's why you owe your soul the responsibility of development and discipline. The soul is intermingled with the spirit to the point that both are sometimes referred to as one. Your soul is your imagination power. With your soul, you can imagine things that don't exist. Everything you see around you was created from the souls of those who invented them. Developing your soul is very important for your well-being. God recreated your spirit; you have to use the characters of your recreated spirit and the Word of God to train your soul. As you know, a Christian is supposed to live from the inside out. If you don't make a conscious decision to do that, your body will gain mastery and affect your soul negatively, which ultimately damages your recreated spirit. That way, you are living from the outside in, and the result is death. You are not supposed to live by your emotions. You don't act or say what you feel. You don't allow your emotions to rule your life. You only live by what the Word of God says, irrespective of how you feel.

The Body

The body is the outward man we see; it is the house of your human spirit and soul. Your body is your legal access to planet earth. Without being in a body, no spirit being is allowed to carry out physical activities on planet earth. Your body gives your spirit legal access to function on earth.

Your body is a gift of trust; you owe your body the responsibility of caring for it. If you don't take care of your body and you lose it, you lose your right to the earth. Somebody once said, "When I destroy my body, I will receive a new one when our bodies will be transformed". Read your bible very well; your current body will first be raised back to life and then transformed. That means you will always have this body. The body has no will; it's either a slave to the five senses or the spirit.

Bringing The Body Under Subjection

We should daily ensure that we bring the body under the subjection of the Word of God. Your body is not yet saved like your spirit is; therefore, the desires of the spirit are contrary to the desires of the body. The Bible says the spirit war against the flesh (the body) and the body war against the spirit. Since the body is not yet saved, you have to make sure you bring the body under subjection to the word of God. Train your body to conform to the desires of your spirit. Let your body only do what the Word of God says, not what it feels like doing. The desire of the body is death to your entire being.

Galatians 5:17-18 For the flesh lusts against the Spirit, and the Spirit against the flesh; and these are contrary to one another, so that you do not do the things that you wish. ¹⁸ But if you are led by the Spirit, you are not under the law.

Galatians 5:19-21 shows us the works of the flesh. In other words, those are the characters of the flesh. You will see the manifestations of those things if you allow your body to rule you. The works of the flesh are death. Look at the works of the flesh below.

Galatians 5:19-21 (GNT) What human nature does is quite plain. It shows itself in immoral, filthy, and indecent actions; ²⁰ in worship of idols and witchcraft. People become enemies and they fight; they become jealous, angry, and ambitious.

They separate into parties and groups; [21] they are envious, get drunk, have orgies, and do other things like these. I warn you now as I have before: those who do these things will not possess the Kingdom of God.

The Fruit Of The Recreated Human Spirit

Instead of your body doing the evil works listed above, your spirit is supposed to bear the fruit of righteousness. When you read Galatians 5:22-23 in most Bible translations, they translated it as though it's the fruits of the Holy Spirit. It is rather fruit to be borne by your born-again spirit. The fruit of your born-again spirit are the characters you develop as a result of your relationship and fellowship with the Holy Spirit and fellow Christians. These characters are developed as a result of consistent feeding on God's word.

Galatians 5:22-24 But the Holy Spirit produces this

kind of fruit in our lives: love, joy, peace, patience, kindness, goodness, faithfulness, [23] gentleness, and self-control. There is no law against these things! [24] Those who belong to Christ Jesus have nailed the passions and desires of their sinful nature to his cross and crucified them there. The more of those fruits you can see in your life, the higher the evidence of your growth as a Christian.

Renew Your Mind With The Word

The word of God is living and active; it can renew the mind and influence the soul. A Christian doesn't need deliverance; what most Christians need is the renewal of the mind to think in a godly way. When you gave your life to Christ, you were translated from the kingdom of darkness into God's kingdom *(Colossians 1:13)*, and that is the kingdom you belong to now. Satan has no authority over you anymore, so you don't need to be delivered from him. Use the Word of God to change your mind and your ways of doing things. Think and see things from God's perspective. It's a daily task and your responsibility until you come to the fullness of God.

It's very easy to renew your mind with Word. Just do whatever the Word says. If the Word says to go to church, go to church. If the Word says to love one another, walk in love towards all men. That is how you will soon manifest the God in you.

Chapter Twelve

The Person of the Holy Spirit

Ihope you are enjoying this book so far. This section is even going to be more interesting. I believe God is teaching you many things through the book. It's time to introduce you to the most important person on planet earth today; the Holy Spirit. He is the author of the Bible and even this book. Let's discuss the person of the Holy Spirit as a subject.

The Holy Spirit Is God Himself

The subject of the Trinity is one of the misunderstood subjects in Christianity. I don't know how the church could miss the revelation of the Holy Spirit since he is the one responsible for all we are as

Christians today. The scope of this book can only introduce us to the basic revelation and knowledge about the person of the Holy Spirit. Much can't be known about the Holy Spirit if you don't have a relationship with him. You will know him better when you have a good relationship with him. The richer the relationship, the better you will know him.

The Godhead

The term Godhead refers to the person of God the Father, God the Son, and God the Holy Spirit. They are also referred to as the Trinity. Trinity simply means three persons in one. The Trinity of God being three persons in one is correct but the explanation is usually incorrect. Many explain the term trinity as three persons working together as one body, that is, three in one. That gives a picture of God the Father, God the Son, and God the Holy Spirit being three different entities working together to achieve a common goal. This idea came from the misunderstanding of a phrase Paul and even Peter used in their expression of the current position of Jesus in heaven. Let me show you the verses.

1 Peter 3:22 Now He has entered heaven and sits at <u>the right hand of God</u> as heavenly messengers and authorities and powers submit to His supremacy.

Hebrews 1:3-4 After making purification for sins, he [Jesus] sat down at <u>the right hand of the Majesty on high</u>

Ephesians 1:20–23 [God] raised [Christ] from the dead and seated him <u>at his right hand</u> in the heavenly places

Hebrews 12:1-2 Looking unto Jesus, the [a]author and finisher of our faith, who for the joy that was set before Him endured the cross, despising the shame, and has sat down at <u>the right hand of the throne of God.</u>

Take note of the underlined phrases. The phrases in all those scriptures above say Jesus is seated "at the right hand of God" and not "at the right-hand side of God" Read those verses again before reading my explanation below.

Being at the right hand of God and being at the right-hand side of God are not the same. When we say someone is seated at your right hand, the person is then your right-hand man. Your right-hand man is a person who represents to the point everything he says or does is you saying or doing it. It means you have given all your authority to the person to act on your behalf. Jesus seated at the right hand of God means he has been given a place of authority and power. It means God has given Jesus all his authority and power which is exactly the reality.

The right-hand side of someone is the geographical location of the opposite of the left-hand side. Jesus is not seated at the opposite of God's left-hand side in heaven. Jesus is not seated on another throne different from that of God in heaven.

Never imagine Jesus seated on a smaller throne beside God on his right-hand side in heaven. When you get to heaven, you will see Jesus on the throne of the Father, not on another throne. When you imagine Jesus as a separate person on another throne besides God, you will then have The Father and Jesus as two separate beings. I once heard of this funny set-up in heaven about the Godhead. The Father is seated on his throne, Jesus seated on a smaller throne beside him and the Holy Spirit flying as a dove above the two of them. That is a very bad picture of the Godhead. That is the source of the explanation of the Godhead being three different personalities working together as Gods.

The Trinity is not three different personalities coming together to work as one body. For better understanding, look at the Trinity as One in Three instead of Three in One. One in three means God the Father, manifesting himself in three different forms or as three different personalities. No matter how you look at the Godhead, He is one. Everything "God" has to do with the Father. That's why we pray to the Father, worship the Father, give our offerings to the Father, sin against the Father, and make our requests to the Father. It's the Father who expressed himself as the Son (Jesus). That is the meaning of "Son of God" Son of God means God the Father in human flesh. Same for the Holy Spirit, The Holy Spirit is God the Father proceeding from himself (duplicating himself) Can you see the Son and the Spirit are all the Father in a different form? The Trinity is then God the Father manifesting himself in three different forms; One in three.

You will get more clarity about this topic in the sections below. Now you understand what we mean by the Holy Spirit is God himself.

The Holy Spirit Is A Person

The Holy Spirit is a person because he has the features of a person. He looks like you; He talks, has a body, has a will, laughs, gets angry, can be grieved, feels happy, has a wish, etc. Genesis 1:26. Man was created in the image of God who is the same as the Holy Spirit.

The Holy Spirit as a person is a revelation the church has not known for a very long time. The church saw the great power of the Holy Spirit, mighty miracles, signs, and wonders, but never knew the person behind all those happenings. Nobody took the time to find out who could be behind the miracles. The church knew it was the Holy Spirit but never knew who he was.

The Holy Spirit lives in and relates with us because he is a person. Knowing the Holy Spirit as a person will make a big difference in your life. The best revelation a man can ever have about the Holy Spirit is to know him as a person. The Holy Spirit is always described in the Bible as a person. From Genesis 1:26, we are told that we were created in the image of God. If we were created "a person", God should also be a person. He has a body and his body is the body of Jesus. The Bible says the Godhead dwells in Jesus bodily.

Now that you know he is a person, it's your responsibility to relate with him as a person. You must first be conscious of his presence in and with you. Talk with him, talk to him, ask for his help, and seek his advice. Allow his ministry in your life. He is the best friend you can ever have. If you are not in a relationship with him, it could be the reason for most of the challenges you might be facing. Friendship with the Holy Spirit can prevent you from many life challenges as he will guide you away from what could be a problem to you. Get into friendship with him today and enjoy that rich fellowship no human can ever give you.

Every Christian Can Receive The Holy Spirit

Nobody can live the authentic Christian life without the Holy Spirit because He enables you to live the supernatural life and do supernatural things *(Acts 1:8)*. He is the one who starts Christianity in you. In the Old Testament, they never had the Holy Spirit live inside them. He only came upon some of them, used them to accomplish a task, and left. In the New

Testament, the Holy Spirit lives inside us 24/7. That has always been God's desire; to live inside man. You may say "but I know people who were filled with the Holy Spirit even from their mother's womb in the Old Testament. Well, to be filled with the Holy Spirit is different from the Holy Spirit dwelling in you. The differences between the indwelling and the infilling of the Spirit are explained below; keep reading.

The Holy Spirit Proceeds From The Father

This is one of the greatest revelations I have ever had about the Holy Spirit. It's the key to my understanding of the Godhead.

John 15:26: The Holy Ghost testifies of Jesus Christ. Jesus taught that "when the Comforter is come, whom I will send unto you from the Father, even the Spirit of truth, which <u>proceedeth</u> from the Father, he shall testify of me

The Godhead (the Father, Son, and the Spirit) are one and are referred to as the Trinity. Our understanding of the oneness of the Godhead is so important to our dealing with them. If you encounter the Father, you have encountered the totality of the Godhead; if you meet the Son, you have encountered the totality of the Godhead; if you met the Spirit, you have encountered the totality of Godhead.

When God talks, his Word carries his personality, character, and nature of him. The Word can then function independently of the Father. The totality of the Father manifests himself in his Word (the Son). As I pointed out above, our prayer, worship, giving, and services are all done to the Father.

God the Father is the one we always refer to as God and he is always on His throne in heaven. God the Father never leaves his throne. When he wants to do something at point **A**, He proceeds out of himself to that point **A** and remains on the throne. When He wants to do something at point **B**, he doesn't need to move from point **A** to **B**, he proceeds again from the throne to point **B** while still at point A and remains on the throne. As the Father on the throne proceeds, he doesn't diminish, because he proceeds many times, he remains the same. When he wants to do something again at point **C**, the one at point **B** can proceed from himself to point **C** and all of them have the same power, authority, personality, character, and nature as the one on the throne. The one that proceeds from the Father carries all the fullness of the Father so that He can be independent of the one on the throne. The one who proceeded from the Father can also proceed from himself to another location. The one that proceeds from the Father is who we call the Holy Spirit (John 15:26). I believe it's clear now how the Holy Spirit is the same as the Father.

From the day of Pentecost, when the Holy Spirit came to start his ministry in the earth, the Father stopped proceeding from himself. He now proceeds from us, glory to God. When the apostles received the Holy Spirit and went to evangelise, the Holy

Spirit proceeded from them to fill the new converts till it got to us today. When I pray for somebody to receive Christ, the Holy Spirit doesn't come from heaven to fill the person, he proceeds out of me to fill the person. What a privilege! The Father can now trust you with the Holy Spirit.

Same for the Word; when the Father talks, his Word carries his full personality, nature and character. Receiving the Word is receiving the Father. Any time the Word and the Spirit proceed out of the Father, they could be so independent to the point that they have their own will. Even though they could have their own will and function independently of the Father, they chose to always subject their will to the will of the Father. When Jesus was born, he had his will, but he chose to do the will of the Father. Jesus said the same thing about the Holy Spirit.

John 16:13 However, when He, the Spirit of truth, has come, He will guide you into all truth; for He will not speak on His own authority, but whatever He hears He will speak; and He will tell you things

to come.

The same thing is required of us; to subject our wills to that of the Father. You have your will and can do anything you want, but the Father wants you to willingly subject your will to his. He wants you to do what he commanded, not what you feel like doing. The will of man is death, but the will of the Father is life.

The Holy Spirit Is The Doer Of The Godhead

The Godhead functions with the principle of division of labour. They play different roles to accomplish the will of the Father. God the Father is the initiator of the ideas. He is the one who comes out with what he wants to accomplish. It's his will and desire. He is the one who formulates the plans, wishes, visions, wills, and ideas.

The Word (the Son) is the idea formulated. A person's words are the articulations of his thoughts, will, wishes, vision, ideas, plans, etc. We know Jesus is the Word of God. That means receiving Jesus Christ is awakening to the Fatherhood of God's plan, will, desire, vision, etc. for your life. Let's define the Word of God in simple terms. ***The word of God is God's vision, plan, wish, desire, and idea in Christ Jesus concerning a person, a place, or a thing.***

The Word of God has been designed to work within the domain of Christ. That is why a man only finds his real purpose when he gives his life to Christ and has been brought into Christ.

The Holy Spirit is the implementer of the will, wish, desire, plan, and vision of God. All God the Father needs is to formulate the plan; the Holy Spirit, the doer, will bring it to pass. In Genesis 1:2, when the Father said, "let there be light," and there was light, it was the Holy Spirit who brought the light into existence. The Holy Spirit is the power of God, the accomplisher of God's will and plan. Have you realised God cannot do anything without His Spirit and His Word? That is why you must not be ignorant of the Holy Spirit in your life. The Holy Spirit doesn't do anything by himself; he only does the will of the Father.

The Name Of The Holy Spirit Is Jesus

Let me ask you a question. What is the real name of the Spirit of God? I heard someone say "Holy Spirit" and others say Holy Ghost. Well, none of those are his name; those are his descriptions. We call him "Holy Spirit" which means "the Spirit who is Holy". As you know, we have different kinds of spirits. The Godhead is a spirit, angels are spirits, demons are spirits, Satan is a spirit, and all humans are spirits.

The Holy Spirit distinguishes himself from all these spirits by his holiness. He is the holiest of all spirits, so we call him Holy Spirit, the spirit who is holy. So, as you can see, Holy Spirit is not his name; it's a description of his personality. What then is his name? His name is Jesus; he answers to the same name Jesus. When you mention Jesus, the Holy Spirit responds. Same for the Father. The Father is not his name, it's his description. The Father is also called Jesus. The name of the Godhead is Jesus. Instead of addressing them individually, you can call them Jesus. Jesus here means the name with all authority and power.

The Difference Between Holy Spirit And Holy Ghost

The terms Holy Spirit and Holy Ghost refer to the same person; the Spirit of God. The difference is the King James translation of the Bible. The King James version of the Bible uses the term Holy Ghost to describe the Spirit of God instead of Holy Spirit as found in all other translations. You can only find the term "Holy Ghost" in the King James version of the Bible and not in any other translation.

Holy Ghost is not a proper rendering of his name because the Spirit of God is not a ghost that is holy. Let's look at what a ghost is. A ghost is the spirit of a dead person. The King James translators used Holy Ghost instead of Holy Spirit because, during those days, they didn't have a good revelation of spirits. They thought a spirit was the same as a ghost. In many ancient writings, they used ghost to mean spirit. They later discovered that a spirit is not the same as a ghost. Of course, every ghost is a spirit, but not all spirits are ghosts.

The Holy Spirit doesn't mind if you call him Holy Ghost with revelation. You can call somebody's name wrongly, but it's still him if you are talking in light of him. Don't worry if you are already so used to calling him Holy Ghost, but calling him with a higher revelation which is Jesus is better.

The Holy Spirit Is The Third Personality Of The Godhead

The Holy Spirit being the third person of the Godhead doesn't mean he is the least among them. It's referring to their dispensation of dealing with men. In the Old Testament, everything was addressed to God the Father. You will see phrases like God said, God spoke to, God visited, God commanded, etc. God in those verses refers to the Father. God the Father was the first among the Godhead to deal with men and, therefore, became the first Person of the Godhead. The dispensation of the Father came to an end when Jesus was born.

The Son became the second of the Godhead to deal with men. When Jesus was born, the Father never said or did anything again. If you needed God, you must go to Jesus. It was the time of the Son. A time came when Jesus said, "It's better for me to go, but when I go, another person will come", talking about the Holy Spirit.

When Jesus ascended, the Holy Spirit came 10 days after to begin his work as the third person of the Godhead. The Holy Spirit then is the third and the last person of the Godhead to carry out his ministry in the earth. From the day of Pentecost, the Holy Spirit has been here with us and will always be with us till the end of the church age.

The Holy Spirit Was In The Old Testament

When you study through the Old Testament portion of the Bible, you will notice the presence and the activities of the Holy Spirit. He played a very vital role in the Old Testament. His works in the Old Testament were so remarkable. At that time, they had no revelation of him because he wasn't properly introduced to the Old Testament people. The reason could be because it was the dispensation of the Father and not the Holy Spirit, so all the activities of the Holy Spirit were still attributed to the Father. A careful study of the Old Testament reveals the activities of the Holy Spirit.

He was the fourth person in the fire with Shadrach, Meshach and Abednego; He was the Angel (messenger) of God's presence Isaiah 63:9; he was that wind that departed the red sea; he was the angel that appeared to Joshua, etc. Anything God wants to do, he does it through the Holy Spirit. The fact that he wasn't directly mentioned in the Old Testament doesn't mean he wasn't there; he was there in his fullness.

The Holy Spirit Can Take Any Form

We have already established that the Holy Spirit is a Person, but he can manifest himself in any form or shape of his choice. For example, an angel, dove, smoke, wind, burning bush, human being etc. The Holy Spirit is none of those, but those are ways he announces his presence to usually draw the attention of people. Never mistake the announcement of his presence to be his person.

Holy Spirit announced his presence to some people with a feel of cold sensation, others felt heat, some say electric current but the same presence of the same Spirit. The smoke, dove, wind, electric current, and all other experiences people had of him are all ways he announces his presence at a place, but he is a person. Do not mistake the person of the Holy Spirit with any form he might announce his presence with.

Deuteronomy 4:15 Take careful heed to yourselves, for you saw no form when the LORD spoke to you at Horeb out of the midst of the fire, [16] lest you act corruptly and make for yourselves a carved image in the form of any figure: the likeness of male or female,

Today, many Christians out of ignorance likened the Holy Spirit and Jesus to some kind of images in their minds. Some of these images have been printed out and hung in their cars and rooms. Look at the verse I read to you above. God warned the children of Israel not to liken him to any image because they saw no form when he appeared to them. God intentionally showed them no form because he knew they would create graven images in that form and worship it. He didn't want them to give him a form, not because he doesn't have one, but because he is a person who will be hard for them to understand under the Old Testament. Learn to express your faith in God without any physical image of him. Christianity is the expressing your faith in the unseen. God doesn't want you to put your faith in printed images of any kind of him. When dealing with the Holy Spirit, don't wait to see a smoke, a wind, a voice, a dove, or anything sign. He is in you.

Chapter Thirteen

Who The Holy Spirit is to You

The Holy Spirit wasn't given to you so you can speak in tongues and feel good. He came for a purpose. He has specific work to do in you, with you and for you. It's your responsibility to work with him to achieve his purpose in you. He is a gentle spirit; he won't force himself on you or against your will. In this chapter, we will study 7 things the Holy Spirit is to you. Oh hallelujah!

John 14:16 And I will pray the Father, and he shall give you another __Comforter__, that he may abide with you forever;

The word translated comforter above comes with seven synonyms in the original translation, which are the works the Holy Spirit will do for us. Let's look at that verse from the Amplified translation.

John 14:16 AMPC And I will ask the Father, and He will give you another Comforter (Counselor, Helper, Intercessor, Advocate, Strengthener, teacher and Standby), that He may remain with you forever—

1. The Holy Spirit Is Your Counselor

Your decisions can make or unmake you. That is why the Holy Spirit was given to counsel you on your decisions.

Proverbs 14:12 There is a way which seemeth right unto a man, But the end thereof are the ways of death.

We make decisions based on the information available to us. Sometimes, that information may be wrong or insufficient to make a sound decision. Also, the decision may be good for now, but the end is a disaster. That is why we need someone who can tell the end from the beginning. The Holy Spirit counsels you on matters and their outcome on your life and the lives of others. He opens your eyes to see how a particular decision is going to affect you and others positively or negatively and tells you the right way to go about it. He is the Spirit who knows everything, he can tell the end from the beginning and, therefore, is the best person to counsel you. Men can't give you the best counsel on life matters since their knowledge is limited. Nobody listens to the counsel of the Holy Spirit and walks in confusion. Turn to him for counsel. Subject your decisions to his counsel.

Remember, after his counsel, the final decision is yours. Therefore, you will have to enjoy or suffer the consequences. Seek his advice on major decisions like your job, church, where to live, whom to marry etc. Follow his counsel and don't make any shortsighted decision based on what you can only see now. His counsel considers eternity and therefore is the best for you.

2. *The Holy Spirit Is Your Helper*

You can't live the Christian life all by yourself; you need the Holy Spirit to help you. If you wouldn't need help, God wouldn't give you a helper. He came to help you pray and serve the Father the way you should. He came to help you know the Father, help you express his nature in you, and walk in his fullness. He was given to help you through the Christian journey. Just allow him, and he will help you. If you find the Christian life difficult, you might have been doing it all by yourself. Yield yourself to him; he came with God's plan for your life; allow him to build you according to the master plan.

3. *The Holy Spirit Is Your Strengthener*

The Holy Spirit strengthens you never to give up on your faith irrespective of what you face. There may be challenges you may encounter along your Christian journey that may make you feel like giving up. Sometimes, voices and circumstances question your faith. Life becomes frustrating at that moment of your life when you are growing your faith, and it seems not to be working. Maybe your life contradicts what you believed. In your weak and tough times, the Holy Spirit strengthens you. He came to strengthen you to wait on God, endure, face the challenges, go through tough times, and win. He gives you the guarantee and gives you strength to run the race to the end *(Philip 4:13)*

4. The Holy Spirit Is Your Intercessor

Praying to God and interceding for others is a service that follows principles. When praying to God, have you ever wondered what at all to tell a God who knows everything? Have you ever thought of what could be the best thing to intercede for when praying for others? The natural man doesn't have enough knowledge to communicate with a God of all-knowing. For this cause, the Holy Spirit was given to us to help us communicate in the language of the Spirit with the Father. We call it speaking in other tongues. As we pray with tongues, the Holy Spirit gives you utterance according to God's will. It's a serious problem when a Christian doesn't speak in tongues. Get my other books on prayer and learn more about the subject of prayer. The Holy Spirit helps intercede for you by putting words of tongues in your mouth to utter to God. He gives you accurate words for every moment and enables you to pray according to the will of God. He doesn't pray for you; he enables you to pray. He joins you in your prayer to help you pray in the right direction.

Romans 8:26 (NIV) In the same way, the Spirit helps us in our weakness. We do not know what we ought to pray for, but the Spirit himself intercedes for us through wordless groans. [27] And he who searches our hearts knows the mind of the Spirit, because the Spirit intercedes for God's people in accordance with the will of God.

Wow, the Holy Spirit helps us groan. Of course, you don't groan when you don't speak in tongues. No wonder those who speak in tongues can pray long, discuss matters with God, and achieve great results. Let him help you pray, and you will always have an answer to your prayers.

If you don't speak in tongues, seek to speak in tongues immediately. It will help you a lot. Go to your pastor and tell him you want to speak in tongues, and he will pray for you to receive the language of the Spirit.

5. The Holy Spirit Is Your Teacher

Since the Holy Spirit is all-knowing, he is the best person to teach anybody anything. Concerning the Word of God, he is the author of the Bible and many other great books of this world. Isaiah, Daniel, Moses, Paul, Peter John and others are just the recorders of the Bible. He was the one who gave the message to record. He is the best person to teach you the scriptures. Put in a conscious effort to learn the Word of God, and you will be amazed at the things he will teach you. I love to read my Bible because the Holy Spirit opens my eyes to see great things in the Bible. The Holy Spirit taught me things I never heard any preacher talk about. One other exciting thing about the Holy Spirit; our teacher is that he doesn't only teach us the scriptures; he can teach you anything, including how to brush your teeth. He can teach you the simplest things no man can teach you. He knows more about you than you know about yourself. He is concerned about every detail of your life, including your hairstyle. He wants you sound and perfect. Yield yourself to his teaching ministry, obey his teachings, and have the best of life.

6. He Is Your Standby

You will understand how the Holy Spirit is our standby better if you know how standby generators work. Standby generators are installed to take over when the main electric power supply goes out. We have the automatic type and the manual type. The automatic type turns on automatically when the main power supply goes out. For the manual type, you need to turn on the key to start it. These generators are usually installed in hospitals and places where the power supply must not be interrupted. The Holy Spirit works for us in the same way.

He is the standby generator, and you are the main power supply. He takes over and supplies you when you are out of strength, wisdom, ideas, faith, etc. Just as the standby generator doesn't turn on when the main power supply is on, the Holy Spirit doesn't supply you with what you have already. He only takes over when you need it. God doesn't expect you to look up to men for anything because men can't help you. He is your standby, whenever you lack strength, courage, ideas, vision, faith, or anything, switch to the supply of the Holy Spirit. Isn't it amazing how God gave us a standby despite all the gifts and abilities he gave us? What a loving God we serve!

7. *The Holy Spirit Is Your Advocate*

Advocate here means one called to go along with you. It also means one called to speak on your behalf. The Holy Spirit is the lawyer who defends you. He performs the role of a lawyer in your life in heavenly and earthly matters. When Satan accuses you before God, he is the one who speaks on your behalf. Whenever you do something wrong, he takes over the matter to make sure your status as a child of God remains untouched. Wherever your name is mentioned, the Holy Spirit your lawyer responds on your behalf. He handles all your legal matters, so you don't need to worry about judgment and condemnation. He has never lost any case.

The Old Testament saints didn't have such privilege, so they always had to face God's judgment for their offences, but we are born again and have the holy spirit defending us all the time. Our wrongdoings couldn't be counted against us; thank God for the Holy Spirit.

Infilling And Indwelling Of The Holy Spirit

1. The Infilling Of The Holy Spirit

We know that before a man gives his life to Christ, he is a child of the Devil, and God has no control over him until he accepts Christ into his life. When he accepts Christ, the authority over his life changes, and God becomes his father and has the right to influence his life now. From the moment he gives his life to Christ, he will start receiving influences like the stir of the Holy Spirit inside him to do supernatural things and to live right. At this point, he might still not have the Spirit permanently dwelling in him but the Spirit of God can use you to do anything.

When you give your life to Christ, that's the first level you go with the Spirit, his influence. That was what the Old Testament people experienced; the coming upon of the Holy Spirit. This coming upon is what we call the infilling of the Holy Spirit. To receive the indwelling of the Holy Spirit, a conscious or unconscious invitation must be made. He must be invited to come make his home in you.

The infilling is the first experience. That is when the Holy Spirit receives you into him. The infilling is when the Holy Spirit receives you into the body of Christ. The infilling is when the Holy Spirit starts his ministry in you as a Christian. It's the coming upon of the Holy Spirit. That was what the Old Testament people experienced but not the indwelling. The Spirit of God came on them to prophesy, to fight in a war, etc., and went away; he didn't permanently dwell in them.

When your pastor lays hands on you, you receive the infilling of the Spirit (impartation of blessings and gifts). When you fast and pray, you receive the infilling; when the Word of God is ministered to you, you receive the infilling. All the activities that stir the power of God in your life are the infillings of the Spirit. You can experience this over and over in different dimensions. It's not a once-in-a-lifetime experience thing. It's something you will experience from time to time in different dimensions.

2. The Indwelling Of The Holy Spirit

This is once and for a lifetime experience. That is the person of the Holy Spirit coming to permanently make his home inside you. He comes, never to go again. This experience may not necessarily happen the same moment a person gives his life to Christ, even though it does happen. This takes a conscious invitation for him to make his home in you. No man of God can lay hands on you for you to receive the indwelling of the Holy Spirit. After the indwelling, you still need constant infilling (the stirring of him) daily. God's dream for you is to have his Spirit permanently dwell in you, not just fill you up for supernatural things.

John 14:15-17 If you love Me, keep My commandments. [16] And I will pray the Father, and He will give you another Helper, that He may abide with you forever [17] the Spirit of truth, whom the world cannot receive, because it neither sees Him nor knows Him; but you know Him, for He dwells with you and will be in you.

In Acts 8:17, Acts 19:6, and other places in the book of Acts, you will read that the apostles laid hands on the new converts; they received the Holy Spirit and prophesied. Most new converts might have only received the infilling of the Spirit, even though the Holy Spirit came upon them and they prophesied. This happened to many Christians as well. They once spoke in tongues and manifested some supernatural abilities, but after some days, they couldn't do any of those things again.

When you have the indwelling, every moment of your life is supernatural. When the Holy Spirit dwells in you, life is different, the search comes to an end and the confusion is over. The big difference between the infilling and the indwelling of the Holy Spirit is the indwelling is for your personal Christian life relationship with the Godhead but the infilling which is also called empowerment for service is for service to others.

The Holy Spirit Is God To You

The Holy Spirit is God giving himself to you. At your new birth, God almighty proceeded out of himself in his totality to reside in you. He came and super-mingled with your spirit that both of you are inseparable. It's you and him till eternality. He will never leave you, no matter what you do. You may say what if I do bad things? That's why he came to help you stop the bad stuff. He only leaves you when you deny Christ; when you accept another lord over your life.

Before Jesus left, the apostles were sad and wondering how they would live without Jesus. But when they received the Holy Spirit, they never missed Jesus. Through the Holy Spirit, they were constantly connected to the Father and the Son.

Receiving the Holy Spirit is receiving the Father and Jesus in fullness into you.

The Holy Spirit Brought You The Nature Of God

The nature of man was corrupted by the fall of Adam. The fallen nature brought about characters like wickedness, envy, jealousy, death, and all those mentioned in Galatians 5:19-21. Man became capable of destroying himself. When you gave your life to Christ, God gave you his nature *(love, mercy, kindness, righteousness, forgiveness, etc.)*. You received the very life of God into you. You can now see situations from God's perspective. That is what makes you seize to be a human. You are now a god.

Now, you can reason and communicate like God. You can express all the qualities of God as well. You can love, be kind, forgive and be righteous like God. It's your responsibility to activate and walk in this new nature. You have to decide to walk in love and righteousness and be kind and good to others. You can read Galatians 5:22-23 to discover the new characters of your new nature. I also explain them in a section below.

Chapter Fourteen

The Impartations of the Spirit

The previous chapter introduced us to the person of the Holy Spirit. Now we will look at His impartation through his power, anointing, his gifts and the fruits he bears in us. These are his working in us to become the image of Christ that God expects from us. They are also his empowerment to impact others with his power at work in us.

The Person And The Power Of The Holy Spirit

For more than 1500 years after the Holy Spirit came to start his ministry, the church only knew his power and not the Person. The church has witnessed the power of the Holy Spirit in several ways but never knew the person behind the miracles, signs, healings, and wonders. It's recently that the church got to know about the person of the Holy Spirit and that has made a big difference in the body of Christ. The Holy Spirit is a person; he is God. He is the power of God.

The power of the Holy Spirit is his influence in a man's life. Through the power of the Holy Spirit, you discover and walk in the new nature you received and express the supernatural. Many only knew the power of the Holy Spirit to be that invasive force that causes people to fall or perform miracles. But the first way a Christian experiences the power of the Holy Spirit is through the transformations he brings into you. His inner workings in you. How he builds and changes you to conform to the image of Christ. His power can make the worst sinner become the best of God.

His power is the things he does inside and through you. His power causes you to manifest and walk in the supernatural. The power of the Holy Spirit can be experienced in different ways healing power, saving power, miracle power, etc. The power of the holy spirit can be experienced without the person of the Holy Spirit. Anything (living or non-living) can experience the power of the Holy Spirit.

Acts 19:11-12 (KJV) And God wrought special miracles by the hands of Paul: [12] So that from his body were brought unto the sick handkerchiefs or aprons, and the diseases departed from them, and the evil spirits went out of them.

The healing power of the Holy Spirit was transported in handkerchiefs and aprons from Paul to the sick, and they got healed. It was the power that was carried in those handkerchiefs and aprons, not the person. In the Old Testament, the anointing oil was the medium used to transport the power of God from one place to the other. The power was imparted to the oil, and whoever came into contact with the oil came into contact with the power of God. Today in the New Testament era, your body is the best vessel to transport the power of God and not the anointing oil. You are the perfect vessel to carry his person, presence, and power. When you received the Holy Spirit, he came with all his fullness and power. That's why it's not appropriate to cry out to God for more power after his Spirit came inside of you. When you need power, stir the Spirit inside you to generate power.

The Anointing Of The Holy Spirit

The anointing of the Holy Spirit is his empowerment, enablement, talents, and abilities impacted to you. These are the abilities he leaves you with. Anytime a person is anointed, he must see himself walking in a new ability. You don't get anointed and remain the same; you were anointed to do something. You might not have been trained for that thing, but the anointing you have received will cause you to do it supernaturally.

Every child of God is anointed to do something. There is a special anointing God gave every believer to do something in his house and for others. Since the things of God need high precision, he always gives his children special abilities to handle them. Some were anointed to clean the church, arrange the chairs, preach, counsel, sing, dance, usher, take care of kids in church, etc.

We often think it's only the men of God who are anointed. Yes, our men and women of God have special anointing upon their lives to offer special services to God's children. You also have a special anointing to provide service(s) to others or in the house of God. To be anointed is to be empowered to do something. If you believe you are anointed, use it to do whatever you are anointed for. Identify what God has anointed you to do and do it diligently.

Some Terminologies and their meaning

Terminology	*Meaning*
Holy Spirit or Holy Ghost	The person of the Spirit of God
The Power of the Holy Spirit	His influence or transformation in a Christian or at a place
The anointing of the Holy Spirit	His empowerment, enablement, and abilities

The Holy Spirit Is Our Sanctifier

This section is very important, and I want you to pay attention to it. You will get the full meaning of sanctification in my other book titled Christian Terminologies. But I want to relate the topic to the Holy Spirit here. One of the biggest differences between the Old Testament and the New Testament is the method of cleansing. The Old Testament had a very complicated system of cleansing, unlike the New Testament. Have you wondered why in the New Testament, we don't need to do all those washings the Jews did to cleans themselves and the vessels. Under the Old Covenant, the Jew had to ceremonially wash himself before he entered the temple. They had to ceremonially wash a plate before they ate on it by sprinkling water on it. The idea is to cleans it or make it sanctify it. In the New Testament, we don't need to do any of those things to be cleansed because we have a different cleansing system. Before God can use or accept anything from the earthly realm, it has to be sanctified. To be sanctified means to be cleansed or washed pure ceremonially for God's use. Things offered to God without being sanctified were rejected by him and most times those who offered it faced severe consequences. That should let you know the importance of sanctification.

In the Old Testament, the altar of sacrifice and the altar in the temple were used to purify or cleanse whatever was offered to God. There was also ceremonial washing to sanctify people and some other things before God. Everything used in the service of God must come into contact with the altar. That's why the animals and the incense must be sacrificed and burnt on the altar to be sanctified. In the temple, the vessels were on the altar; offerings were given to God on the altar.

In the New Testament, God is no longer in the temple; he is now inside us. We don't need the altar to sanctify our works to God anymore. The Holy Spirit is our sanctifying mechanism in the New Testament. He was given to us to sanctify our works. This is one of the reasons why receiving the Holy Spirit is important. You couldn't offer anything to God without the Holy Spirit. He is the one who sanctifies our services, offerings, prayers, bodies, works, etc., to be accepted by God. That is why we don't need all those ceremonial cleansings in the New Testament. The sanctifier himself is now inside us. We are constantly sanctified and presented before God blameless.

Colossians 1:22 (NIV) But now he has reconciled you by Christ's physical body through death to present you holy in his sight, without blemish and

Glory be to our Lord Jesus Christ, who loved us so much and gave himself for us. Lord, we are grateful.

The Gifts Of The Holy Spirit

The Holy Spirit as a person is a gift to you from the Father (Acts 2:38-39). When he came, he also brought some wonderful gifts to you. The gifts of the Holy Spirit refer to his manifestations in the life of a Christian for the profit of others. These gifts can be received by an unbeliever for the sake of a believer. These are not gifts to pastors or those who pray a lot; they are gifts every believer can receive when needed.

These gifts are different from the offices or the callings in Ephesians 4:11 *(pastor, prophet, apostle, evangelist, and teacher)* given to the church. Those are special callings on the life of some people for the perfection of the saints. For example, there is a gift of prophecy (*gift of the Spirit*) and there is an office of the prophet (*the office*). Every child of God can receive the gift of prophecy, but every child of God cannot be called into the office of the prophet.

1 Corinthians 14:1 Pursue love, and desire spiritual gifts, but especially that you may prophesy.

It's God's dream for all his children to prophesy, but he never wants all of us in the office of the prophet. The gifts of the Holy Spirit are given when they are desired or demanded. For example, if there is a sick person, whoever desires the gift of healing can be given that gift to heal the sick at that moment. It's the same for all the gifts. You can receive any of them by desire and faith. These gifts are:

1 Corinthians 12:7-11 But the manifestation of the Spirit is given to each one for the profit of all: [8] for to one is given <u>the word of wisdom</u> through the Spirit, to another <u>the word of knowledge</u> through the same Spirit, [9] to another <u>faith</u> by the same Spirit, to another <u>gifts of healings</u> by the same

Spirit, [10] to another the <u>working of miracles</u>, to another <u>prophecy</u>, to another <u>discerning of spirits</u>, to another <u>different kinds of tongues</u>, to another the <u>interpretation of tongues</u>. [11] But one and the same Spirit works all these things, distributing to each one individually as he wills.

The Gifts Of The Holy Spirit And The Fruit Of The Born-Again Spirit

The gifts of the Holy Spirit are given for the edifying and building of the body of Christ. They are gifts to be used to the benefit of all. They can be desired and received through faith 1 Cor 12:7-10. The gifts of the Holy Spirit are given by the Spirit of God, and it's for service to others.

The fruits of the spirit (the born-again spirit) refer to the characters developed by the recreated human spirit as a result of fellowship with the Holy Spirit and other believers. Galatians 5:22-23. You are the one to develop the fruits; they are not giftings you receive from the Holy Spirit or the Father. For example, one of the fruits is patience. If you are quick-tempered, it's your responsibility to develop patience with the help of the power of the holy spirit inside you and the Word of God. You don't pray to God for patience. So are all the fruits. They don't come by prayer or as a gift from the Holy Spirit.

In conclusion, we just discussed the Holy Spirit is a person, and therefore we have to relate to him as a person. He came into your life for a purpose. You have to go into fellowship with him. He is the gentlest person on earth today and doesn't force himself on anybody. He came to help you do the work God has given you; he didn't come to do the work for you. Start doing everything you must do as a Christian, and let him help you. Encourage his ministry in you and allow him to do his work in your life.

Don't live a helpless life as though you were never given a helper. Don't live your life as an orphan because Jesus said he wouldn't leave us as one

(John 14:18). If you haven't seen all these beautiful ministries of the Spirit in your life, either you are not born again or you have been ignorant of him. I want you to know that if you have received the Holy Spirit, He will always be with you and never leave you irrespective of your behaviour. God knows how you are, so He sent him to help you. Just talk to him and make your life upright with Him again. Life is full of mysteries without the Holy Spirit. I never wish such a life for you; it's too expensive. I highly recommend the Holy Spirit to you today. If you are not born again, turn to the next page of the book and pray the prayer of salvation and you be saved. If you are already born again but don't have the Holy Spirit, turn to the next pages and pray the prayer to receive the Holy Spirit and he will come right away to live in you. Glory to God!

I highly recommend you read this book over and over. You can just pick a chapter and read over it or a sub-title and read for better understanding. This book contains too much information that can't be absorbed by reading it once. I pray the God of our Lord Jesus Christ bless you with the Spirit of understanding and wisdom to know his will and purpose for you. May God's Spirit help and strengthen your faith in him and give you the grace to accomplish every assignment he has given you, in Jesus' name. Amen

PRAYER OF SALVATION

If you are not born again and would like to receive the Lord Jesus into your heart, pray the prayer below and believe from the bottom of your heart.

Dear Lord Jesus, I believe with all my heart that you came to die for my sins and on the third day, God raised you from the dead. through your resurrection, the full penalty for my sins was paid. This day, I invite you to be my Lord and personal saviour. I declare that am saved, am born again and the name of Jesus Christ is named upon me. I receive eternal life into my heart. Thank you, Jesus, for saving me and making me a king and priest unto God the Father. Amen

PRAYER FOR THE HOLY SPIRIT

Now in case, after reading this portion on the Holy Spirit, and it seems like you don't have the Holy Spirit, don't worry. He is right there with you and waiting for your invitation. Just pray this simple prayer, and you will have him right away.

Dear Holy Spirit of God, thank you for getting this book to me with which you taught me about yourself. I love you and need your full ministry in my life. I invite you to make your home in me, to be the Lord of my spirit, soul, and body. I am ready to yield myself to you in everything. By faith, I receive you into my heart. Thank you for coming into my heart. As I fellowship with you, I know my life will never be the same in Jesus' mighty name. Amen

You have just received him. Be conscious of his presence and talk to him like any friend. You don't need to feel anything, but I can guarantee you, you will start seeing his works in your life. Congratulation!

OTHER BOOKS BY THE AUTHOR

1. Fundamental Doctrines of Christ
2. Faith Hall of Fame
3. Higher Dimensions of Prayer
4. Christian Terminologies
5. Audacity of Faith
6. Lessons from Isaac's Family
7. The Mystery of the Church
8. Divine Health
9. Our Oneness with the Lord Jesus
10. How to Raise a Child the Way He Should Go

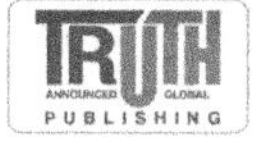 *Truth Announced Global Publishing*

Contacts

If you want copies of this book, call or WhatsApp any of these numbers close to you or send us email with emails bellow.

China	Wechat ID: Deguols
Southern Africa	+267-72899582
Ghana	+233-557628424
Zambia	+260-962387631
Uganda	+256-709725309
South Sudan	+211-918417929

Copies are also available on Amazon

Emails:

truthannounced@gmail.com
Deguols@gmail.com